VERSATILE KNITWEAR DESIGNS FOR PLUS SIZES

CLASSIC KNITS FOR REAL WOMEN

MARTIN STOREY AND SHARON BRANT
PHOTOGRAPHS BY PETER WILLIAMS

VERSATILE KNITWEAR DESIGNS FOR PLUS SIZES

CLASSIC KNITS FOR REAL WOMEN

MARTIN STOREY AND SHARON BRANT
PHOTOGRAPHS BY PETER WILLIAMS

C&T PUBLISHING

First published in North America by
C&T Publishing Inc.,
PO Box 1456, Lafayette, CA 94549

Copyright © Rowan Yarns 2005

Art direction, styling, and design by
Georgina Rhodes and **Richard Proctor**
Editor **Sally Harding**
Pattern writer **Sue Whiting**
Pattern checker **Stella Smith**

British Library Cataloging in Publication Data
A catalog record of this book is available from
the British Library

ISBN 1-57120-369-9
Printed in Singapore

CONTENTS

INTRODUCTION

Not all women are 18 years old and a size 8, and few knitting pattern books give sizes beyond a 14. The purpose of this book is to offer a range of great designs for women of all ages, in sizes that start at size 12.

Women who love to knit, like all women, often lead quite complex lives: working, caring for children in many cases, and, with luck and if not too tired, enjoying a social life as well. With this in mind, the designs in this book are, first and foremost, adaptable. You can dress them up or down. You can wear them aged 20, 40, or 60 plus. You can wear them walking the dog or pushing the stroller, or to the office, or for a night out after work.

The jacket shown on page 11 (above far left) looks great worn casually with the sleeves pushed up in the daytime, but would also dress up for an evening out when worn over the sleeveless top shown on page 21.

We realize that one length or one style does not suit all, so the designs offer a range of hip lengths and neck styles. Some come in alternative versions, such as the top with a round or a V-neck (on pages 59 and 105), allowing you to choose what suits you best.

We selected three flattering, go-anywhere, color palettes—one of cool blues, grays, and blacks, another of subtle neutrals and naturals, and a third of warmer, richer autumnal shades— in a range of classic Rowan and Jaeger yarns that work across our increasingly confusing seasons!

In keeping with our desire to create designs that real people could wear, we photographed the knitwear in this book without using professional models (a testament to the talent of Peter Williams, the photographer). We are indebted to the women (of varying ages and sizes) who took time out of their busy lives to model the clothes for us and also complemented them with clothes from their own wardrobes: so a truly heartfelt thanks to Marian, Jan, Molly, Bluebell, Poppy, Kristy, and Sally. You looked great wearing them and, more importantly, you seemed to enjoy the experience!

Martin Storey and Sharon Brant

COOL COLORS

This clear, spring-like color palette
goes with many different colors, but
is particularly good teamed with gray,
white, navy, and black, and is great for
the summer, too. It is flattering to wear
for most skin tones and hair colors.
Designs in this section include several
great jackets—some dressy, some
casual—and evening sweaters and
tops in a great selection of yarn types
and weights.

Left *The Fringe-trim Coat is wonderfully versatile and very flattering. Knitted in a chunky merino wool yarn, it is both soft and really warm. Wear it with jeans for country walks or dress it up for town with dark gray trousers and a camisole. (Instructions on page 24.)*

Right *Worked in lightweight merino wool, this great Houndstooth Jacket takes its inspiration from Chanel's classic box shape. Its softly harmonizing gray and pale plum checks are worked in the Fair Isle technique. The cabled trim around the collar and cuffs adds a sophisticated finish. (Instructions on page 26.)*

Above The combination of denim yarn with beads is ideal for both dressing up and down. Here, the Bead-trellis Jacket looks great worn casually with jeans, but would work equally well for the evening, with a beaded camisole (see page 21) underneath. (Instructions on page 29.)

Right Making this long-line Cable Guernsey is a great way to show off your knitting skills! It is knitted in denim yarn and has a flattering high neck. (Instructions on page 32.)

Right The Scallop-trim Jacket is knitted in an Aran-weight merino yarn, making it the ideal choice for the fall or for cool spring days. Great as a casual cover up for the country, it also translates effortlessly into a smart jacket for the office. (Instructions on page 36.)

Above (front) The short denim Bead-trellis Scarf takes its theme from the Bead-trellis Jacket (see page 12). Wear it with a smart plain pullover or jacket for maximum effect. (Instructions on page 35.) The Beaded Top in the background is also shown on page 21.

Right This Ruffled V-Neck Sweater is feminine and flattering. Knitted in a lightweight cotton yarn, it is ideal for summer evenings and smart enough to carry on from the office to an evening out. (Instructions on page 40.)

Left *Beaded loops of a mohair-silk yarn create the frothy collar on the Flower-trim Jacket. Worked in a double-knitting merino yarn, the jacket turns into a classic V-neck cardigan if you omit the collar. (Instructions on page 42.)*

Right *This elegant cotton Lace-sleeve Sweater keeps you cool but covers you up. It works well as daytime wear and for evening, too. (Instructions on page 48.)*

Pages 20 and 21
Left *The Textured Jacket is a variation on the Beaded Jacket shown on page 69. Knitted in an extra-fine merino yarn, it is the ideal classic jacket for summer and winter alike. (Instructions on page 96.)*

Center *The Poodle-collar Jacket (shown also on page 22) is really versatile and can be worn either as a cover-up for evening or casually for relaxing, as here.*

Right *Knitted in soft lightweight merino yarn, the Beaded Top looks chic on its own for evening or summer days. It also makes the perfect companion for the Beaded Trellis Jacket on page 12. (Instructions on page 38.)*

Left Worked in luxuriously soft mohair-mix yarn, the Poodle-collar Jacket is a really flattering style to wear. The loop stitch for the collar is quick to master and fun to knit. (Instructions on page 45.)

Above The Cable-yoke Jacket is a design for all ages and all sizes. It has a wonderful chunky texture in denim yarn, and features split sides and a fringed hem and collar. A guaranteed classic! (Instructions on page 50.)

FRINGE-TRIM COAT

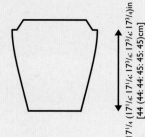

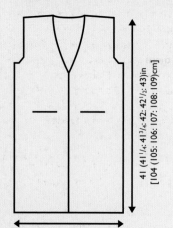

23¹/₂ (24¹/₂: 25¹/₂: 26¹/₂: 27¹/₂: 28¹/₂)in
[59.5 (62: 64.5: 67.5: 70: 72.5)cm]

41 (41¹/₄: 41³/₄: 42: 42¹/₂: 43)in
[104 (105: 106: 107: 108: 109)cm]

17¹/₄ (17¹/₄: 17¹/₄: 17³/₄: 17³/₄: 17³/₄)in
[44 (44: 44: 45: 45: 45)cm]

SIZES

1	2	3	4	5	6

TO FIT BUST

36	38	40	42	44	46	in
91	97	102	107	112	117	cm

YARN

Jaeger Extra Fine Merino Chunky—gray and beige tweed (019)

31	31	32	33	34	35 x 50g

NEEDLES

1 pair size 8 (5mm) needles
1 pair size 10 (6mm) needles
Size 8 (5mm) circular needle
2 double-pointed size 8 (5mm) needles

GAUGE

15 sts and 20 rows to 4in/10cm measured over St st using size 10 (6mm) needles.

BACK

Cast on 89 (93: 97: 101: 105: 109) sts using size 8 (5mm) needles.
Work in garter st for 14 rows, ending with a WS row.
Change to size 10 (6mm) needles.
Beg with a K row, cont in St st until back measures 79 (80: 80: 81: 81: 82)cm/31¼ (31½: 31½: 31¾: 31¾: 32¼)in, ending with a WS row.
Shape armholes
Bind off 3 sts at beg of next 2 rows. 83 (87: 91: 95: 99: 103) sts.
Dec 1 st at each end of next 6 rows. 71 (75: 79: 83: 87: 91) sts.
Work even until armhole measures 9¾ (9¾: 10¼: 10¼: 10¾: 10¾)in/25 (25: 26: 26: 27: 27)cm, ending with a WS row.
Shape shoulders and back neck
Bind off 7 (8: 8: 9: 9: 10) sts at beg of next 2 rows. 57 (59: 63: 65: 69: 71) sts.
Next row (RS): Bind off 7 (8: 8: 9: 9: 10) sts, K until there are 12 (11: 13: 13: 14: 14) sts on right needle and turn, leaving rem sts on a holder.

Work each side of neck separately.
Bind off 4 sts at beg of next row.
Bind off rem 8 (7: 9: 9: 10: 10) sts.
With RS facing, rejoin yarn to rem sts, bind off center 19 (21: 21: 21: 23: 23) sts, K to end.
Complete to match first side, reversing shapings.

POCKET LININGS (make 2)

Cast on 27 sts using size 10 (6mm) needles.
Beg with a K row, work in St st for 36 rows, ending with a WS row.
Break yarn and leave sts on a holder.

LEFT FRONT

Cast on 45 (47: 49: 51: 53: 55) sts using size 8 (5mm) needles.
Work in garter st for 14 rows, ending with a WS row.
Change to size 10 (6mm) needles.
Beg with a K row, cont in St st until left front measures 20¼ (20½: 20½: 20¾: 20¾: 21¼)in/ 51 (52: 52: 53: 53: 54)cm, ending with a WS row.
Place pocket
Next row (RS): K11, slip next 27 sts onto a holder and, in their place, K across 27 sts of first pocket lining, K to end.
Cont in St st until 10 rows less have been worked than on back to beg of armhole shaping, ending with a WS row.
Shape front slope
Dec 1 st at end of next and foll 0 (2: 1: 1: 2: 2) alt rows, then on every foll 4th row until 42 (43: 46: 48: 49: 51) sts rem.
Work 1 (1: 3: 3: 1: 1) rows, ending with a WS row. (Left front now matches back to beg of armhole shaping.)
Shape armhole
Bind off 3 sts at beg and dec 0 (0: 1: 1: 0: 0) st at end of next row. 39 (40: 42: 44: 46: 48) sts.
Work 1 row.
Dec 1 st at armhole edge of next 6 rows **and at same time** dec 1 st at front slope edge on next (next: 3rd: 3rd: next: next) and foll 4th (4th: 0: 0: 4th: 4th) row. 31 (32: 35: 37: 38: 40) sts.

Dec 1 st at front slope edge **only** on 3rd (3rd: next: next: 3rd: 3rd) and every foll 4th row until 22 (23: 25: 27: 28: 30) sts rem. Work even until left front matches back to start of shoulder shaping, ending with a WS row.

Shape shoulder
Bind off 7 (8: 8: 9: 9: 10) sts at beg of next and foll alt row. Work 1 row.
Bind off rem 8 (7: 9: 9: 10: 10) sts.

RIGHT FRONT
Cast on 45 (47: 49: 51: 53: 55) sts using size 8 (5mm) needles.
Work in garter st for 14 rows, ending with a WS row.
Change to size 10 (6mm) needles.
Beg with a K row, cont in St st until right front measures 20¼ (20½: 20½: 20¾: 20¾: 21¼)in/ 51 (52: 52: 53: 53: 54)cm, ending with a WS row.

Place pocket
Next row (RS): K7 (9: 11: 13: 15: 17), slip next 27 sts onto a holder and, in their place, K across 27 sts of second pocket lining, K to end.
Complete to match left front, reversing shapings.

SLEEVES (both alike)
Cast on 43 (45: 45: 47: 49: 49) sts using size 8 (5mm) needles.
Work in garter st for 20 rows, inc 1 st at each end of 5th and every foll 4th row and ending with a WS row. 51 (53: 53: 55: 57: 57) sts.
Change to size 10 (6mm) needles.
Beg with a K row, cont in St st, inc 1 st at each end of next and every foll 4th (6th: 4th: 6th: 6th: 6th) row to 55 (71: 57: 71: 81: 81) sts, then on every foll 6th (8th: 6th: 8th: -: -) row until there are 75 (75: 77: 77: -: -) sts.
Work even until sleeve measures 17¼ (17¼: 17¼: 17¾: 17¾: 17¾)in/44 (44: 44: 45: 45: 45)cm, ending with a WS row.

Shape top of sleeve
Bind off 3 sts at beg of next 2 rows. 69 (69: 71: 71: 75: 75) sts.

Dec 1 st at each end of next and foll 4 alt rows, then on foll row, ending with a WS row. Bind off rem 57 (57: 59: 59: 63: 63) sts.

FINISHING
BLOCK as described on page 123.
Join both shoulder seams using backstitch, or mattress stitch if preferred.

Front bands and collar
With RS facing and using size 8 (5mm) circular needle, starting and ending at cast-on edges, pick up and knit 119 (120: 120: 122: 122: 124) sts up right front opening edge to start of front slope shaping, 40 (40: 42: 43: 44: 45) sts up right front slope to shoulder, 27 (28: 30: 30: 31: 31) sts from back, 40 (40: 42: 43: 44: 45) sts down left front slope to start of front slope shaping, then 119 (120: 120: 122: 122: 124) sts down left front opening edge. 345 (348: 354: 360: 363: 369) sts.
Row 1 (WS of body, RS of collar): K187 (189: 193: 196: 198: 201), wrap next st (by slipping next st onto right needle, taking yarn to opposite side of work between needles and then slipping same st back onto left needle— when working back across wrapped sts, K tog the st and the wrapped loop), turn.
Row 2: K29 (30: 32: 32: 33: 33), wrap next st and turn.
Row 3: K30 (31: 33: 33: 34: 34), wrap next st and turn.
Row 4: K31 (32: 34: 34: 35: 35), wrap next st and turn.
Row 5: K32 (33: 35: 35: 36: 36), wrap next st and turn.
Row 6: K33 (34: 36: 36: 37: 37), wrap next st and turn.
Cont in this way, working one more st before wrapping next st and turning, until the foll row has been worked:
Row 40: K67 (68: 70: 70: 71: 71), wrap next st and turn.
Row 41: K69 (70: 72: 72: 73: 73), wrap next st and turn.
Row 42: K71 (72: 74: 74: 75: 75), wrap next st and turn.

Row 43: K73 (74: 76: 76: 77: 77), wrap next st and turn.
Row 44: K75 (76: 78: 78: 79: 79), wrap next st and turn.
Cont in this way, working 2 more sts before wrapping next st and turning, until the foll row has been worked:
Next row: K107 (108: 114: 114: 119: 119), wrap next st and turn.
Next row: K to end.
Now cont in garter st across all sts until band measures 2in/5cm from pick-up row, measuring at front opening edges, ending with RS of body facing for next row.
Using size 8 (5mm) double-pointed needles, work fringe bind-off as foll: K3, *(without turning slip these 3 sts to opposite end of needle and bring yarn to opposite end of work pulling it quite tightly across WS of work, K these 3 sts again) 16 times, without turning slip these 3 sts to opposite end of needle and bring yarn to opposite end of work pulling it quite tightly across WS of work, K3tog and fasten off, K next 3 sts of band, rep from * until all sts have been bound off.

Pocket tops (both alike)
Slip 27 sts from pocket holder onto size 8 (5mm) needles and rejoin yarn with RS facing.
Work in garter st for 7 rows.
Bind off knitwise (on WS).

See page 124 for finishing instructions, setting in sleeves using the shallow set-in method.

HOUNDSTOOTH JACKET

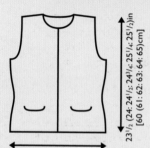

21 (22: 23: 24: 25: 26)in
[53 (55.5: 58: 60.5: 63: 65.5)cm]

23½ (24: 24½: 24¾: 25¼: 25½)in
[60 (61: 62: 63: 64: 65)cm]

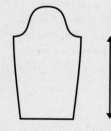

17¼ (17¼: 17¼: 17¾: 17¾: 17¾)in
[44 (44: 44: 45: 45: 45)cm]

SIZES

1	2	3	4	5	6	

TO FIT BUST

36	38	40	42	44	46	in
91	97	102	107	112	117	cm

YARNS

Rowan 4 ply Soft
A gray (384)

7	7	8	8	9	9 x 50g

B light dusty plum (378)

7	7	8	8	9	9 x 50g

NEEDLES

1 pair size 2 (2¾mm) needles
1 pair size 3 (3¼mm) needles
Cable needle

BUTTONS—5

GAUGE

32 sts and 29 rows to 4in/10cm measured over pattern using size 3 (3¼mm) needles.

SPECIAL ABBREVIATIONS

C6B = slip next 3 sts onto cable needle and leave at back of work, K3, then K3 from cable needle.

BACK

Cast on 149 (157: 163: 171: 177: 185) sts using size 2 (2¾mm) needles and yarn A.
Row 1 (RS): K1, *P1, K1, rep from * to end.
Row 2: Rep row 1.
These 2 rows form seed st.
Cont in seed st for a further 11 rows, ending with a RS row.
Row 14 (WS): Seed st 4 (8: 4: 8: 4: 8) sts, M1, *seed st 7 sts, M1, rep from * to last 5 (9: 5: 9: 5: 9) sts, seed st to end. 170 (178: 186: 194: 202: 210) sts.
Change to size 3 (3¼mm) needles.
Join in yarn B.
Starting and ending rows as indicated, using the **Fair Isle** technique as described on page 123

and repeating the 4 row patt rep throughout, cont in patt from chart, which is worked entirely in St st beg with a K row, as foll:
Work 12 rows, ending with a WS row.
Dec 1 st at each end of next and every foll 8th row until 158 (166: 174: 182: 190: 198) sts rem.
Work 9 rows, ending with a WS row.
Inc 1 st at each end of next and every foll 6th row until there are 170 (178: 186: 194: 202: 210) sts, taking inc sts into patt.
Work even until back measures 14½ (15: 15: 15¼: 15½: 15¾)in/37 (38: 38: 39: 39: 40)cm, ending with a WS row.
Shape armholes
Keeping patt correct, bind off 6 (7: 7: 8: 8: 9) sts at beg of next 2 rows. 158 (164: 172: 178: 186: 192) sts.
Dec 1 st at each end of next 9 (9: 11: 11: 13: 13) rows, then on foll 6 (7: 7: 8: 8: 9) alt rows, then on every foll 4th row until 124 (128: 132: 136: 140: 144) sts rem.
Work even until armhole measures 9 (9: 9½: 9½: 9¾: 9¾)in/23 (23: 24: 24: 25: 25)cm, ending with a WS row.
Shape shoulders and back neck
Bind off 12 (12: 13: 14: 14: 15) sts at beg of next 2 rows. 100 (104: 106: 108: 112: 114) sts.
Next row (RS): Bind off 12 (12: 13: 14: 14: 15) sts, patt until there are 16 (17: 17: 17: 18: 18) sts on right needle and turn, leaving rem sts on a holder.
Work each side of neck separately.
Bind off 4 sts at beg of next row.
Bind off rem 12 (13: 13: 13: 14: 14) sts.
With RS facing, rejoin yarns to rem sts, bind off center 44 (46: 46: 46: 48: 48) sts, patt to end.
Complete to match first side, reversing shapings.

LEFT FRONT

Cast on 82 (86: 89: 93: 96: 100) sts using size 2 (2¾mm) needles and yarn A.
Row 1 (RS): *K1, P1, rep from * to last 0 (0: 1: 1: 0: 0) st, K0 (0: 1: 1: 0: 0).
Row 2: K0 (0: 1: 1: 0: 0), *P1, K1, rep from * to end.

These 2 rows form seed st.

Cont in seed st for a further 11 rows, ending with a RS row.

Row 14 (WS): Seed st 8 sts and slip these sts onto a holder, seed st 2 (4: 2: 4: 2: 4) sts, M1, *seed st 7 sts, M1, rep from * to last 2 (4: 2: 4: 2: 4) sts, seed st to end. 85 (89: 93: 97: 101: 105) sts.

Change to size 3 (3¼mm) needles.

Join in yarn B.

Starting and ending rows as indicated, cont in patt from chart as foll:

Work 12 rows, ending with a WS row.

Dec 1 st at beg of next and every foll 8th row until 79 (83: 87: 91: 95: 99) sts rem.

Work 9 rows, ending with a WS row.

Inc 1 st at beg of next and every foll 6th row until there are 85 (89: 93: 97: 101: 105) sts, taking inc sts into patt.

Work even until left front matches back to beg of armhole shaping, ending with a WS row.

Shape armhole

Keeping patt correct, bind off 6 (7: 7: 8: 8: 9) sts at beg of next row. 79 (82: 86: 89: 93: 96) sts.

Work 1 row.

Dec 1 st at armhole edge of next 9 (9: 11: 11: 13: 13) rows, then on foll 6 (7: 7: 8: 8: 9) alt rows, then on every foll 4th row until 62 (64: 66: 68: 70: 72) sts rem.

Work even until 15 (15: 15: 15: 15: 17) rows less have been worked than on back to start of shoulder shaping, ending with a RS row.

Shape neck

Keeping patt correct, bind off 8 (9: 9: 9: 10: 9)

sts at beg of next row, then 9 sts at beg of foll alt row. 45 (46: 48: 50: 51: 54) sts.

Dec 1 st at neck edge of next 6 rows, then on foll 3 (3: 3: 3: 3: 4) alt rows, ending with a WS row. 36 (37: 39: 41: 42: 44) sts.

Shape shoulder

Bind off 12 (12: 13: 14: 14: 15) sts at beg of next and foll alt row.

Work 1 row.

Bind off rem 12 (13: 13: 13: 14: 14) sts.

RIGHT FRONT

Cast on 82 (86: 89: 93: 96: 100) sts using size 2 (2¾mm) needles and yarn A.

Row 1 (RS): K0 (0: 1: 1: 0: 0), *P1, K1, rep from * to end.

Row 2: *K1, P1, rep from * to last 0 (0: 1: 1: 0: 0) st, K0 (0: 1: 1: 0: 0).

These 2 rows form seed st.

Cont in seed st for a further 11 rows, ending with a RS row.

Row 14 (WS): Seed st 2 (4: 2: 4: 2: 4) sts, M1, *seed st 7 sts, M1, rep from * to last 10 (12: 10: 12: 10: 12) sts, seed st 2 (4: 2: 4: 2: 4) sts and turn, leaving rem 8 sts on a holder. 85 (89: 93: 97: 101: 105) sts.

Change to size 3 (3¼mm) needles.

Join in yarn B.

Starting and ending rows as indicated, cont in patt from chart as foll:

Work 12 rows, ending with a WS row.

Dec 1 st at end of next and every foll 8th row until 79 (83: 87: 91: 95: 99) sts rem.

Complete to match left front, reversing shapings.

SLEEVES (both alike)

Cast on 78 (80: 80: 82: 84: 84) sts using size 3 (3¼mm) needles and yarn A.

Join in yarn B.

Starting and ending rows as indicated, cont in patt from chart, inc 1 st at each end of 5th and every foll 4th row to 108 (110: 116: 116: 118: 124) sts, then on every foll 6th row until there are 124 (126: 128: 130: 132: 134) sts, taking inc sts into patt.

Work even until sleeve measures 16½ (16½: 16½: 17: 17: 17)in/42 (42: 42: 43: 43: 43)cm, ending with a WS row.

Shape sleeve cap

Keeping patt correct, bind off 6 (7: 7: 8: 8: 9) sts at beg of next 2 rows. 112 (112: 114: 114: 116: 116) sts.

Dec 1 st at each end of next 11 rows, then every foll alt row to 74 sts, then on foll 11 rows, ending with a WS row. 52 sts.

Bind off 5 sts at beg of next 4 rows.

Bind off rem 32 sts.

FINISHING

BLOCK as described on page 123.

Join both shoulder seams using backstitch, or mattress stitch if preferred.

Left front band

Slip 8 sts from left front holder onto size 2 (2¾mm) needles and rejoin yarn A with RS facing.

Cont in seed st as set until band, when slightly stretched, fits up left front opening edge to neck shaping, ending with a WS row.

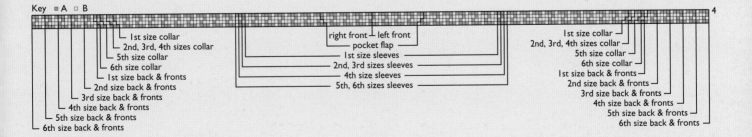

Key ■ A □ B

— 1st size collar
— 2nd, 3rd, 4th sizes collar
— 5th size collar
— 6th size collar
— 1st size back & fronts
— 2nd size back & fronts
— 3rd size back & fronts
— 4th size back & fronts
— 5th size back & fronts
— 6th size back & fronts

right front ┐ ┌ left front
pocket flap
— 1st size sleeves
— 2nd, 3rd sizes sleeves
— 4th size sleeves
— 5th, 6th sizes sleeves

1st size collar —
2nd, 3rd, 4th sizes collar —
5th size collar —
6th size collar —
1st size back & fronts —
2nd size back & fronts —
3rd size back & fronts —
4th size back & fronts —
5th size back & fronts —
6th size back & fronts —

Bind off in seed st.

Slip stitch band in place.

Mark positions for 5 buttons on this band section—first to come 3½in/9cm up from cast-on edge, last to come ½in/1cm below neck shaping, and rem 3 buttons evenly spaced between.

Right front band

Slip 8 sts from right front holder onto size 2 (2¾mm) needles and rejoin yarn A with WS facing.

Cont in seed st as set until band, when slightly stretched, fits up right front opening edge to neck shaping, ending with a WS row and with the addition of 5 buttonholes worked as foll:

Buttonhole row (RS): Seed st 2 sts, work 2 tog, yo (to make a buttonhole), seed st 4 sts.

Bind off in seed st.

Slip stitch band in place.

Collar

Cast on 156 (160: 160: 160: 164: 168) sts using size 3 (3¼mm) needles and yarn A.

Join in yarn B.

Starting and ending rows as indicated, cont in patt from chart as foll:

Work 1 row, ending with a RS row.

Inc 1 st at each end of next 2 rows, taking inc sts into patt. 160 (164: 164: 164: 168: 172) sts.

Work a further 27 rows, ending with a WS row.

Bind off 20 (21: 21: 21: 21: 22) sts at beg of next 4 rows.

Bind off rem 80 (80: 80: 80: 84: 84) sts.

Pocket flaps (make 2)

Cast on 28 sts using size 3 (3¼mm) needles and yarn A.

Join in yarn B.

Starting and ending rows as indicated, cont in patt from chart as foll:

Work 1 row, ending with a RS row.

Inc 1 st at each end of next 2 rows, taking inc sts into patt. 32 sts.

Work a further 9 rows, ending with a WS row.

Bind off.

Cuff edging (both alike)

Cast on 8 sts using size 2 (2¾mm) needles and yarn A.

Row 1 (RS): P2, K6.

Row 2: P6, K2.

Row 3: P2, C6B.

Row 4: Rep row 2.

Rows 5 and 6: Rep rows 1 and 2.

These 6 rows form patt.

Cont in patt until cuff edging fits across cast-on edge of sleeve, ending with a WS row.

Bind off.

Slip stitch un-cabled edge to cast-on edge of sleeve.

Collar edging

Cast on 8 sts using size 2 (2¾mm) needles and yarn A.

Cont in patt as given for cuff edging until collar edging fits around entire row-end and cast-on edges of collar, ending with a WS row.

Bind off.

Slip stitch un-cabled edge in place.

Pocket flap edgings (both alike)

Cast on 8 sts using size 2 (2¾mm) needles and yarn A.

Cont in patt as given for cuff edging until pocket flap edging fits around entire row-end and cast-on edges of pocket flap, ending with a WS row.

Bind off.

Slip stitch un-cabled edge in place.

Sew shaped bound-off edge of collar to neck edge, positioning row-end edge of collar edging halfway across top of front bands.

Using photograph as a guide, sew bound-off edge of pocket flaps to fronts.

See page 124 for finishing instructions, setting in sleeves using the set-in method.

BEAD-TRELLIS JACKET

22¹/₂ (23¹/₂: 24¹/₂: 25¹/₂: 26¹/₂: 27¹/₂)in
[57.5 (59.5: 62.5: 64.5: 67.5: 69.5)cm]

24 (24¹/₂: 24³/₄: 25¹/₄: 25¹/₂: 26)in
[61 (62: 63: 64: 65: 66)cm]

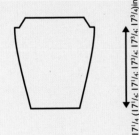

17¹/₄ (17¹/₄: 17¹/₄: 17³/₄: 17³/₄: 17³/₄)in
[44 (44: 44: 45: 45: 45)cm]

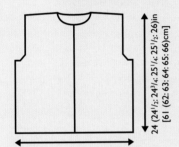

SIZES

1	2	3	4	5	6

TO FIT BUST

| 36 | 38 | 40 | 42 | 44 | 46 | in |
| 91 | 97 | 102 | 107 | 112 | 117 | cm |

YARN

Rowan Denim—dark blue (229)

18	19	20	21	22	23 x 50g

NEEDLES

1 pair size 3 (3¹/₄mm) needles
1 pair size 6 (4mm) needles

BUTTONS—6

BEADS—2,020 (2,130: 2,330: 2,400: 2,660: 2,740) 3mm clear glass beads (Rowan J3000-01008)

GAUGE

Before washing: 20 sts and 28 rows to 4in/10cm measured over St st using size 6 (4mm) needles.

Gauge note: Denim will shrink in length when washed for the first time. Allowances have been made in the pattern for shrinkage (see size diagram on the left for after-washing measurements).

SPECIAL ABBREVIATION

bead 1 = place a bead by bringing yarn to RS of work and slipping bead up next to st just worked, slip next st purlwise from left needle to right needle and take yarn to WS of work, leaving bead sitting on RS of work in front of slipped st. Do not place beads on edge stitches of work as this will interfere with seams.

Pattern note: Before starting to knit, thread beads onto yarn. To do this, thread a fine sewing needle (one that will easily pass through the beads) with sewing thread. Knot ends of thread and then pass end of yarn through this loop. Thread a bead onto sewing thread and then gently slide it along and onto knitting yarn. Continue in this way until required number of beads are on yarn.

BACK

Cast on 115 (119: 125: 129: 135: 139) sts using size 3 (3¹/₄mm) needles.
Work in garter st for 12 rows, ending with a WS row.
Change to size 6 (4mm) needles.
Row 13 (RS): Knit.
Row 14: K5, P to last 5 sts, K5.
Rep last 2 rows 10 times more.
Beg with a K row, cont in St st until back measures 17¹/₄ (17³/₄: 18: 18¹/₄: 18¹/₄: 18³/₄)in/44.5 (45.5: 45.5: 46.5: 46.5: 48)cm, ending with a WS row.
Shape armholes
Bind off 6 sts at beg of next 2 rows. 103 (107: 113: 117: 123: 127) sts.
Dec 1 st at each end of next and foll 2 alt rows. 97 (101: 107: 111: 117: 121) sts.
Work 1 row, ending with a WS row.
Beg and ending rows as indicated and rep the 16 row patt rep throughout, cont in patt from chart as foll:
Dec 1 st at each end of next and foll 2 alt rows. 91 (95: 101: 105: 111: 115) sts.
Work even until armhole measures 10³/₄ (10³/₄: 11: 11: 11¹/₂: 11¹/₂)in/27 (27: 28: 28: 29: 29)cm, ending with a WS row.
Shape shoulders and back neck
Bind off 10 (11: 12: 12: 13: 14) sts at beg of next 2 rows. 71 (73: 77: 81: 85: 87) sts.
Next row (RS): Bind off 10 (11: 12: 12: 13: 14) sts, patt until there are 15 (14: 15: 17: 17: 17) sts on right needle and turn, leaving rem sts on a holder.
Work each side of neck separately.
Bind off 4 sts at beg of next row.
Bind off rem 11 (10: 11: 13: 13: 13) sts.
With RS facing, rejoin yarn to rem sts, bind off center 21 (23: 23: 23: 25: 25) sts, patt to end.
Complete to match first side, reversing shapings.

LEFT FRONT

Cast on 66 (68: 71: 73: 76: 78) sts using size 3 (3¼mm) needles.

Work in garter st for 11 rows, ending with a RS row.

Row 12 (WS): K8 and slip these sts onto a holder, K to end. 58 (60: 63: 65: 68: 70) sts.

Change to size 6 (4mm) needles.

Row 13 (RS): Knit.

Row 14: P to last 5 sts, K5.

Rep last 2 rows 10 times more.

Beg with a K row, cont in St st until left front matches back to beg of armhole shaping, ending with a WS row.

Shape armhole

Bind off 6 sts at beg of next row. 52 (54: 57: 59: 62: 64) sts.

Work 1 row.

Dec 1 st at armhole edge of next and foll 2 alt rows. 49 (51: 54: 56: 59: 61) sts.

Work 1 row, ending with a WS row.

Beg and ending rows as indicated, cont in patt from chart as foll:

Dec 1 st at armhole edge of next and foll 2 alt rows. 46 (48: 51: 53: 56: 58) sts.

Work even until 15 (17: 17: 17: 17: 17) rows less have been worked than on back to start of shoulder shaping, ending with a RS row.

Shape neck

Bind off 7 (7: 7: 7: 8: 8) sts at beg of next row. 39 (41: 44: 46: 48: 50) sts.

Dec 1 st at neck edge of next 4 rows, then on foll 3 (4: 4: 4: 4: 4) alt rows, then on foll 4th row, ending with a WS row. 31 (32: 35: 37: 39: 41) sts.

Shape shoulder

Bind off 10 (11: 12: 12: 13: 14) sts at beg of next and foll alt row.

Work 1 row.

Bind off rem 11 (10: 11: 13: 13: 13) sts.

RIGHT FRONT

Cast on 66 (68: 71: 73: 76: 78) sts using size 3 (3¼mm) needles.

Work in garter st for 4 rows, ending with a WS row.

Row 5 (RS): K3, K2tog, yo (to make a buttonhole), K to end.

Work in garter st for a further 6 rows, ending with a RS row.

Row 12 (WS): K to last 8 sts and turn, leaving rem 8 sts on a holder. 58 (60: 63: 65: 68: 70) sts.

Change to size 6 (4mm) needles.

Row 13 (RS): Knit.

Row 14: K5, P to end.

Complete to match left front, reversing shapings.

SLEEVES (both alike)

Cast on 51 (53: 53: 55: 57: 57) sts using size 3 (3¼mm) needles.

Work in garter st for 12 rows, ending with a WS row.

Change to size 6 (4mm) needles.

Beg with a K row, cont in St st, inc 1 st at each end of next and every foll 4th (6th: 4th: 6th: 4th: 4th) row to 55 (89: 63: 97: 65: 65) sts, then on every foll 6th (8th: 6th: -: 6th: 6th) row until there are 93 (93: 97: -: 101: 101) sts.

Work even until sleeve measures 20¼ (20¼: 20¼: 20¾: 20¾: 20¾)in/51.5 (51.5: 51.5: 52.5:

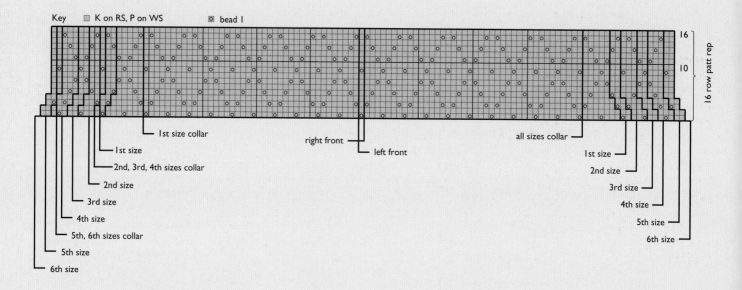

Key   ☐ K on RS, P on WS   ◙ bead 1

16

10

16 row patt rep

1st size collar

1st size

2nd, 3rd, 4th sizes collar

2nd size

3rd size

4th size

5th, 6th sizes collar

5th size

6th size

right front

left front

all sizes collar

1st size

2nd size

3rd size

4th size

5th size

6th size

52.5: 52.5)cm, ending with a WS row.

Shape top of sleeve

Bind off 6 sts at beg of next 2 rows. 81 (81: 85: 85: 89: 89) sts.

Dec 1 st at each end of next and foll 5 alt rows, then on foll row, ending with a WS row.

Bind off rem 67 (67: 71: 71: 75: 75) sts.

FINISHING

Do NOT press.

Join both shoulder seams using backstitch, or mattress stitch if preferred.

Left front band

Slip 8 sts from left front holder onto size 3 (3¼mm) needles and rejoin yarn with RS facing.

Cont in garter st until band, when slightly stretched, fits up left front opening edge to neck shaping, ending with a WS row.

Bind off.

Slip stitch band in place.

Mark positions for 6 buttons on this band section—first to come level with buttonhole already worked in right front, last to come ½in/1cm below neck shaping, and rem 4 buttons evenly spaced between.

Right front band

Slip 8 sts from right front holder onto size 3 (3¼mm) needles and rejoin yarn with WS facing.

Cont in garter st until band, when slightly stretched, fits up right front opening edge to neck shaping, ending with a WS row and with the addition of a further 5 buttonholes worked as foll:

Buttonhole row (RS): K3, K2tog, yo (to make a buttonhole), K3.

When band is complete, bind off.

Slip stitch band in place.

Collar

Cast on 93 (101: 101: 101: 109: 109) sts using size 3 (3¼mm) needles.

Work in garter st for 6 rows, ending with a WS row.

Beg and ending rows as indicated, cont in patt from chart as foll:

Row 7 (RS): K6, work next 81 (89: 89: 89: 97: 97) sts as row 1 of chart, K6.

Row 8: K4, P2, work next 81 (89: 89: 89: 97: 97) sts as row 2 of chart, P2, K4.

These 2 rows set the sts.

Cont as set for a further 30 rows, ending with a WS row.

Bind off 9 (10: 10: 10: 11: 11) sts at beg of next 6 rows.

Bind off rem 39 (41: 41: 41: 43: 43) sts.

Machine wash all pieces before completing sewing together.

Matching ends of collar to center of bands, sew bound-off edge of collar to neck edge.

See page 124 for finishing instructions, setting in sleeves using the shallow set-in method and leaving side seams open for first 34 rows.

CABLE GUERNSEY

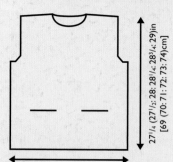

22¹/₂ (23¹/₂: 24¹/₂: 25¹/₂: 26¹/₂: 27¹/₂)in
[57.5 (59.5: 62.5: 64.5: 67.5: 69.5)cm]

27¹/₄ (27¹/₂: 28: 28¹/₄: 28³/₄: 29)in
[69 (70: 71: 72: 73: 74)cm]

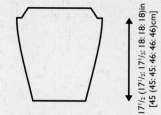

17¹/₂ (17¹/₂: 17¹/₂: 18: 18: 18)in
[45 (45: 45: 46: 46: 46)cm]

SIZES

1	2	3	4	5	6	

TO FIT BUST

36	38	40	42	44	46	in
91	97	102	107	112	117	cm

YARN

Rowan Denim—mid blue (231)

20	21	22	23	24	25 x 50g

NEEDLES

1 pair size 3 (3¹/₄mm) needles
1 pair size 6 (4mm) needles
Cable needle

GAUGE

Before washing: 20 sts and 28 rows to 4in/10cm measured over St st using size 6 (4mm) needles.

Gauge note: Denim will shrink in length when washed for the first time. Allowances have been made in the pattern for shrinkage (see size diagram on the left for after-washing measurements).

SPECIAL ABBREVIATIONS

C4B = slip next 2 sts onto cable needle and leave at back of work, K2, then K2 from cable needle.

C4F = slip next 2 sts onto cable needle and leave at front of work, K2, then K2 from cable needle.

C6B = slip next 3 sts onto cable needle and leave at back of work, K3, then K3 from cable needle.

C6F = slip next 3 sts onto cable needle and leave at front of work, K3, then K3 from cable needle.

BACK

Cast on 115 (119: 125: 129: 135: 139) sts using size 3 (3¹/₄mm) needles.
Row 1 (RS): K1, *P1, K1, rep from * to end.
Row 2: Rep row 1.

These 2 rows form seed st.
Work in rib for a further 7 rows, ending with a RS row.
Row 10 (WS): Seed st 10 (12: 15: 17: 20: 22) sts, M1, (seed st 1 st, M1) twice, seed st 18 sts, M1, (seed st 1 st, M1) twice, seed st 15 sts, M1, (seed st 1 st, M1) twice, seed st 17 sts, M1, (seed st 1 st, M1) twice, seed st 15 sts, M1, (seed st 1 st, M1) twice, seed st 18 sts, M1, (seed st 1 st, M1) twice, seed st to end. 133 (137: 143: 147: 153: 157) sts.
Change to size 6 (4mm) needles.
Cont in patt, placing chart, as foll:
Row 1 (RS): Seed st 6 sts, K1 (3: 6: 8: 11: 13), work next 119 sts as row 1 of chart for body, K1 (3: 6: 8: 11: 13), seed st 6 sts.
Row 2: Seed st 6 sts, P1 (3: 6: 8: 11: 13), work next 119 sts as row 2 of chart for body, P1 (3: 6: 8: 11: 13), seed st 6 sts.
These 2 rows set position of chart.
Keeping sts correct as set, work a further 30 rows, ending with a WS row.**
Now working seed st border sts in ridge patt (but keeping chart correct), work even until back measures 21 (21¹/₂: 21³/₄: 22: 22: 22¹/₄)in 53.5 (55: 55: 56: 56: 57)cm, ending with a WS row.
***Shape armholes
Keeping patt correct, bind off 6 sts at beg of next 2 rows. 121 (125: 131: 135: 141: 145) sts.
Dec 1 st at each end of next and foll 5 alt rows. 109 (113: 119: 123: 129: 133) sts.
Work even until armhole measures 10³/₄ (10³/₄: 11: 11: 11¹/₂: 11¹/₂)in/27 (27: 28: 28: 29: 29)cm, ending with a WS row.
Shape shoulders and back neck
Bind off 12 (12: 13: 14: 14: 15) sts at beg of next 2 rows. 85 (89: 93: 95: 101: 103) sts.
Next row (RS): Bind off 12 (12: 13: 14: 14: 15) sts, patt until there are 15 (16: 17: 17: 19: 19) sts on right needle and turn, leaving rem sts on a holder.
Work each side of neck separately.
Bind off 4 sts at beg of next row.
Bind off rem 11 (12: 13: 13: 15: 15) sts.
With RS facing, rejoin yarn to rem sts, bind off

center 31 (33: 33: 33: 35: 35) sts, patt to end. Complete to match first side, reversing shapings.

POCKET LININGS (make 2)

Cast on 33 sts using size 6 (4mm) needles. Beg with a K row, work in St st for 51 rows, ending with a RS row.

Row 52 (WS): (P11, M1) twice, P11. 35 sts. Break yarn and leave sts on a holder.

FRONT

Work as given for back to **, ending with a WS row.

Now working seed st border sts in ridge patt (but keeping chart correct), work 20 rows, ending with a WS row.

Place pockets

Next row (RS): Patt 15 (17: 20: 22: 25: 27)

sts, slip next 35 sts onto a holder and, in their place, patt across 35 sts of first pocket lining, patt 33 sts, slip next 35 sts onto another holder and, in their place, patt across 35 sts of second pocket lining, patt to end.

Work as given for back from *** until 16 (18: 18: 18: 18: 18) rows less have been worked than on back to start of shoulder shaping, ending with a WS row.

Shape neck

Next row (RS): Patt 44 (46: 49: 51: 53: 55) sts and turn, leaving rem sts on a holder. Work each side of neck separately.

Dec 1 st at neck edge of next 5 rows, then on foll 3 (4: 4: 4: 4: 4) alt rows, then on foll 4th row, ending with a WS row. 35 (36: 39: 41: 43: 45) sts.

Shape shoulder

Bind off 12 (12: 13: 14: 14: 15) sts at beg of

next and foll alt row.

Work 1 row.

Bind off rem 11 (12: 13: 13: 15: 15) sts.

With RS facing, rejoin yarn to rem sts, bind off center 21 (21: 21: 21: 23: 23) sts, patt to end. Complete to match first side, reversing shapings.

SLEEVES (both alike)

Cast on 58 (60: 60: 62: 64: 64) sts using size 3 (3¼mm) needles.

Row 1 (RS): K0 (0: 0: 1: 0: 0), P1 (2: 2: 2: 0: 0), (K2, P2) 3 (3: 3: 3: 4: 4) times, *K4, (P2, K2) twice, P2, rep from * twice more, K2, P1 (2: 2: 2: 2: 2), K0 (0: 0: 1: 2: 2).

Row 2 and every foll alt row: P0 (0: 0: 1: 0: 0), K1 (2: 2: 2: 0: 0), (P2, K2) 3 (3: 3: 3: 4: 4) times, *P4, (K2, P2) twice, K2, rep from * twice more, P2, K1 (2: 2: 2: 2: 2), P0 (0: 0: 1: 2: 2).

Sleeve chart

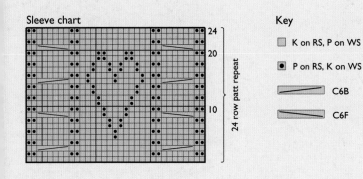

Key

☐ K on RS, P on WS

▣ P on RS, K on WS

▱ C6B

▱ C6F

24 row patt repeat

Body chart

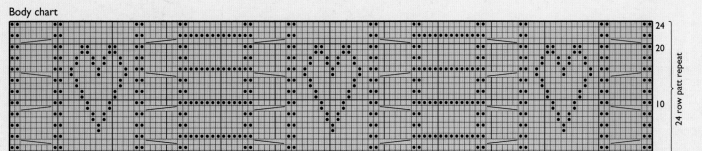

24 row patt repeat

Row 3: K0 (0: 0: 1: 0: 0), P1 (2: 2: 2: 2: 0: 0), (K2, P2) 3 (3: 3: 3: 3: 4: 4) times, *C4B, (P2, K2) twice, P2, rep from * twice more, K2, P1 (2: 2: 2: 2: 2: 2), K0 (0: 0: 1: 2: 2).

Row 5: Rep row 1.

Row 7: K0 (0: 0: 1: 0: 0), P1 (2: 2: 2: 2: 0: 0), (K2, P2) 3 (3: 3: 3: 3: 4: 4) times, *C4F, (P2, K2) twice, P2, rep from * twice more, K2, P1 (2: 2: 2: 2: 2: 2), K0 (0: 0: 1: 2: 2).

Row 8: Rep row 2.

These 8 rows form cabled rib patt.

Cont in cabled rib patt for a further 15 rows, ending with a RS row.

Row 24 (WS): Rib 4 (5: 5: 6: 7: 7), (work 2 tog, rib 10) 4 times, work 2 tog, rib to end. 53 (55: 55: 57: 59: 59) sts.

Change to size 6 (4mm) needles.

Cont in patt, placing chart for sleeve, as foll:

Row 1 (RS): K10 (11: 11: 12: 13: 13), work next 33 sts as row 1 of chart for sleeve, K to end.

Row 2: P10 (11: 11: 12: 13: 13), work next 33 sts as row 2 of chart for sleeve, P to end.

These 2 rows set position of chart.

Keeping chart correct, cont as foll:

Rows 3 and 4: K10 (11: 11: 12: 13: 13), work next 33 sts as chart, K to end.

Row 5: Inc in first st, K9 (10: 10: 11: 12: 12), work next 33 sts as chart, K to last st, inc in last st. 55 (57: 57: 59: 61: 61) sts.

Row 6: P11 (12: 12: 13: 14: 14), work next 33 sts as row 6 of chart, P to end.

This 6 rows set the sts—central chart with ridge patt at sides—and start sleeve shaping.

Cont in patt, inc 1 st at each end of 3rd and every foll 4th row to 81 (77: 89: 83: 91: 91) sts, then on every foll 6th row until there are 99 (99: 103: 103: 107: 107) sts, taking inc sts into ridge patt.

Work even until sleeve measures 20¾ (20¾: 20¾: 21: 21: 21)in/52.5 (52.5: 52.5: 53.5: 53.5: 53.5)cm, ending with a WS row.

Shape top of sleeve

Keeping patt correct, bind off 6 sts at beg of next 2 rows. 87 (87: 91: 91: 95: 95) sts.

Dec 1 st at each end of next and foll 5 alt rows, then on foll row, ending with a WS row. Bind off rem 73 (73: 77: 77: 81: 81) sts.

FINISHING

Do NOT press.

Join right shoulder seam using backstitch, or mattress stitch if preferred.

Collar

With RS facing and using size 3 (3¼mm) needles, pick up and knit 23 (23: 23: 23: 25: 25) sts down left side of neck, 19 (19: 19: 19: 23: 23) sts from front, 23 (23: 23: 23: 25: 25) sts up right side of neck, then 35 (35: 35: 35: 41: 41) sts from back. 100 (100: 100: 100: 114: 114) sts.

Row 1 and every foll alt row (WS): K2, *(P2, K2) twice, P4, K2, rep from * to end.

Row 2: P2, *C4B, (P2, K2) twice, P2, rep from * to end.

Row 4: P2, *K4, (P2, K2) twice, P2, rep from * to end.

Row 6: P2, *C4F, (P2, K2) twice, P2, rep from * to end.

Row 8: Rep row 4.

These 8 rows form cabled rib patt.

Cont in cabled rib patt until collar measures 4¼in/10.5cm, ending with a WS row.

Bind off in patt.

Pocket tops (both alike)

Slip 35 sts from pocket holder onto size 3 (3¼mm) needles and rejoin yarn with RS facing.

Row 1 (RS): (K10, K2tog) twice, K11. 33 sts.

Work in seed st as for back for 9 rows.

Bind off in seed st.

Machine wash all pieces before completing sewing together.

See page 124 for finishing instructions, setting in sleeves using the shallow set-in method and leaving side seams open for first 42 rows.

BEAD-TRELLIS SCARF

YARN
Rowan Denim – mid blue (231)
6 x 50g

NEEDLES
1 pair size 3 (3¼mm) needles
1 pair size 6 (4mm) needles

BEADS
BEADS—approx 2,300 3mm clear glass beads (Rowan J3000-01008)

GAUGE
Before washing: 20 sts and 28 rows to 4in/10cm measured over St st using size 6 (4mm) needles.

Gauge note: Denim will shrink in length when washed for the first time. Allowances have been made in the pattern for shrinkage.

FINISHED SIZE
Completed scarf measures 8in/20.5cm wide and 63in/160cm long.

SPECIAL ABBREVIATION
bead 1 = place a bead by bringing yarn to RS of work and slipping bead up next to st just worked, slip next st purlwise from left needle to right needle and take yarn to WS of work, leaving bead sitting on RS of work in front of slipped st.

Pattern note: Before starting to knit, thread beads onto yarn. To do this, thread a fine sewing needle (one that will easily pass through the beads) with sewing thread. Knot ends of thread and then pass end of yarn through this loop. Thread a bead onto sewing thread and then gently slide it along and onto knitting yarn. Continue in this way until required number of beads are on yarn.

SCARF
Cast on 41 sts using size 3 (3¼mm) needles. Work in garter st for 4 rows, ending with a WS row.
Change to size 6 (4mm) needles.
Next row (RS): Knit.
Next row: K3, P to last 3 sts, K3.
Cont in patt as foll:
Row 1 (RS): K4, (bead 1, K3) 9 times, K1.
Row 2 and every foll alt row: K3, P to last 3 sts, K3.
Row 3: K5, bead 1, (K5, bead 1, K1, bead 1) 3 times, K5, bead 1, K5.
Row 5: K6, (bead 1, K3) 8 times, K3.
Row 7: K7, (bead 1, K1, bead 1, K5) 4 times, K2.
Row 9: Rep row 1.
Row 11: Rep row 7.
Row 13: Rep row 5.
Row 15: Rep row 3.
Row 16: Rep row 2.
These 16 rows form patt.
Rep last 16 rows 31 times more, then rows 1 and 2 again.
Change to size 3 (3¼mm) needles.
Work in garter st for 3 rows.
Bind off knitwise (on WS).

FINISHING
Machine wash as described on ball band, then BLOCK as described on page 123.

SCALLOP-TRIM JACKET

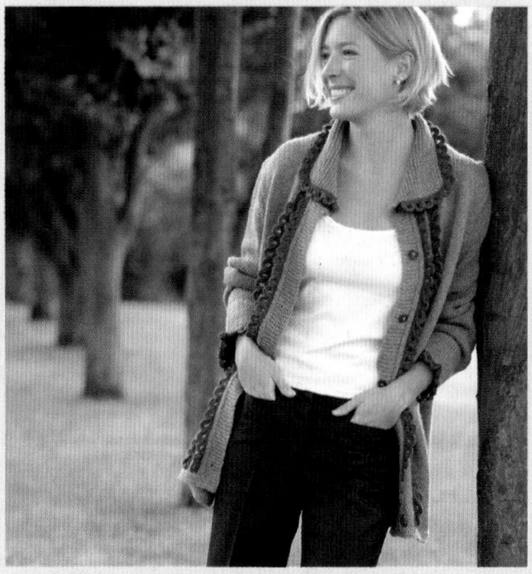

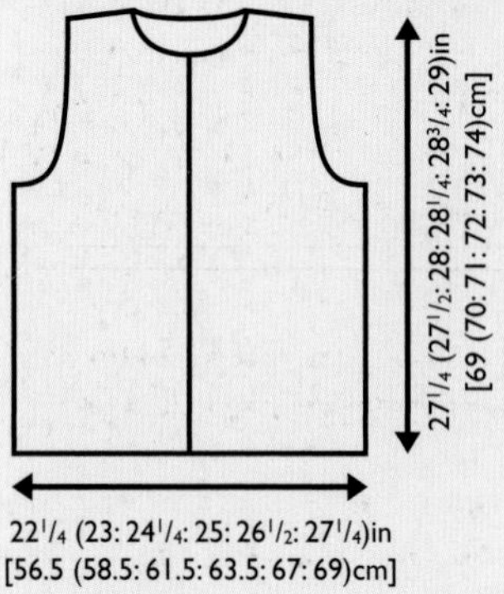
27¼ (27½: 28: 28¼: 28¾: 29)in
[69 (70: 71: 72: 73: 74)cm]
22¼ (23: 24¼: 25: 26½: 27¼)in
[56.5 (58.5: 61.5: 63.5: 67: 69)cm]

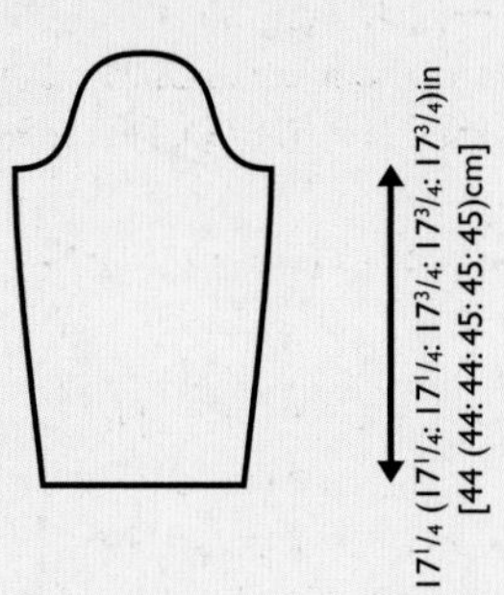
17¼ (17¼: 17¼: 17¾: 17¾: 17¾)in
[44 (44: 44: 45: 45: 45)cm]

SIZES

1	2	3	4	5	6	

TO FIT BUST

36	38	40	42	44	46	in
91	97	102	107	112	117	cm

YARNS

Jaeger Extra Fine Merino Aran

A light gray (542)

17	17	18	19	19	20 x 50g

Extra Fine Merino DK

B gray tweed (978)

1	1	1	1	2	2 x 50g

NEEDLES

1 pair size 3 (3mm) needles
1 pair size 6 (4mm) needles
1 pair size 7 (4½mm) needles

BUTTONS—6

GAUGE

19 sts and 25 rows to 4in/10cm measured over St st using size 7 (4½mm) needles and yarn A.

BACK

Cast on 107 (111: 117: 121: 127: 131) sts using size 6 (4mm) needles and yarn A.
Work in garter st for 6 rows, ending with a WS row. Change to size 7 (4½mm) needles.
Next row (RS): Knit.
Next row: K4, P to last 4 sts, K4.
Rep last 2 rows 13 times more, ending with a WS row.
Beg with a K row, cont in St st until back measures 18¼ (18½: 18½: 19: 19: 19¼)in/46 (47: 47: 48: 48: 49)cm, ending with a WS row.

Shape armholes

Bind off 6 (7: 7: 8: 8: 9) sts at beg of next 2 rows. 95 (97: 103: 105: 111: 113) sts.
Next row (RS): K3, K2tog, K to last 5 sts, K2tog tbl, K3.
Next row: P3, P2tog tbl, P to last 5 sts, P2tog, P3.
Working all armhole decreases as set by last 2 rows, dec 1 st at each end of next 1 (1: 3: 3: 5: 5) rows, then on foll 6 alt rows, then on every foll 4th row until 73 (75: 77: 79: 81: 83) sts rem.
Work even until armhole measures 9 (9: 9½: 9½: 9¾: 9¾)in/23 (23: 24: 24: 25: 25)cm, ending with a WS row.

Shape shoulders and back neck

Bind off 7 (7: 7: 8: 8: 8) sts at beg of next 2 rows. 59 (61: 63: 63: 65: 67) sts.
Next row (RS): Bind off 7 (7: 7: 8: 8: 8) sts, K until there are 11 (11: 12: 11: 11: 12) sts on right needle and turn, leaving rem sts on a holder.
Work each side of neck separately.
Bind off 4 sts at beg of next row.
Bind off rem 7 (7: 8: 7: 7: 8) sts.
With RS facing, rejoin yarn to rem sts, bind off center 23 (25: 25: 25: 27: 27) sts, K to end.
Complete to match first side, reversing shapings.

LEFT FRONT

Cast on 61 (63: 66: 68: 71: 73) sts using size 6 (4mm) needles and yarn A.
Work in garter st for 5 rows, ending with a RS row.
Next row (WS): K7 and slip these 7 sts onto a holder, K to end. 54 (56: 59: 61: 64: 66) sts.
Change to size 7 (4½mm) needles.
Next row (RS): Knit.
Next row: P2, K1, P4, K1, P to last 4 sts, K4.
Rep last 2 rows 13 times more, ending with a WS row.
Next row (RS): Knit.
Next row: P2, K1, P4, K1, P to end.
Last 2 rows form patt.
Cont in patt until left front matches back to beg of armhole shaping, ending with a WS row.

Shape armhole

Keeping patt correct, bind off 6 (7: 7: 8: 8: 9) sts at beg of next row. 48 (49: 52: 53: 56: 57) sts.
Work 1 row.
Working all armhole decreases as set by back, dec 1 st at armhole edge of next 3 (3: 5: 5: 7: 7) rows, then on foll 6 alt rows, then on every foll 4th row until 37 (38: 39: 40: 41: 42) sts rem.

Work even until 13 (13: 13: 13: 13: 15) rows less have been worked than on back to start of shoulder shaping, ending with a RS row.

Shape neck

Bind off 8 (9: 9: 9: 10: 9) sts at beg of next row. 29 (29: 30: 31: 31: 33) sts.

Dec 1 st at neck edge of next 6 rows, then on foll 1 (1: 1: 1: 1: 2) alt rows, then on foll 4th row, ending with a WS row. 21 (21: 22: 23: 23: 24) sts.

Shape shoulder

Bind off 7 (7: 7: 8: 8: 8) sts at beg of next and foll alt row.

Work 1 row.

Bind off rem 7 (7: 8: 7: 7: 8) sts.

RIGHT FRONT

Cast on 61 (63: 66: 68: 71: 73) sts using size 6 (4mm) needles and yarn A.

Work in garter st for 5 rows, ending with a RS row.

Next row (WS): K to last 7 sts and turn, leaving rem 7 sts on a holder. 54 (56: 59: 61: 64: 66) sts.

Change to size 7 (4½mm) needles.

Next row (RS): Knit.

Next row: K4, P to last 8 sts, K1, P4, K1, P2.

Rep last 2 rows 13 times more, ending with a WS row.

Next row (RS): Knit.

Next row: P to last 8 sts, K1, P4, K1, P2.

Last 2 rows form patt.

Complete to match left front, reversing shapings.

SLEEVES (both alike)

Cast on 49 (51: 51: 53: 55: 55) sts using size 7 (4½mm) needles and yarn A.

Beg with a K row, cont in St st, inc 1 st at each end of 5th and every foll 6th row to 55 (57: 65: 65: 67: 75) sts, then on every foll 8th row until there are 73 (75: 77: 79: 81: 83) sts.

Work even until sleeve measures 16 (16: 16: 16½: 16½: 16½)in/41 (41: 41: 42: 42: 42)cm, ending with a WS row.

Shape sleeve cap

Bind off 6 (7: 7: 8: 8: 9) sts at beg of next 2 rows. 61 (61: 63: 63: 65: 65) sts.

Working all decreases as set by back and front armholes, dec 1 st at each end of next 5 rows, then on foll 6 alt rows, then on every foll 4th row until 35 (35: 37: 37: 39: 39) sts rem.

Work 1 row, ending with a WS row.

Dec 1 st at each end of next and every foll alt row to 29 sts, then on foll 5 rows, ending with a WS row. Bind off rem 19 sts.

FINISHING

BLOCK as described on page 123.

Join both shoulder seams using backstitch, or mattress stitch if preferred.

Left front band

Slip 7 sts from left front holder onto size 6 (4mm) needles and rejoin yarn A with RS facing.

Cont in garter st until band, when slightly stretched, fits up left front opening edge to neck shaping, ending with a WS row.

Break yarn and leave sts on a holder.

Slip stitch band in place.

Mark positions for 6 buttons on this band section—first to come 2in/5cm up from cast-on edge, last to come just above neck shaping, and rem 4 buttons evenly spaced between.

Right front band

Slip 7 sts from right front holder onto size 6 (4mm) needles and rejoin yarn A with WS facing.

Cont in garter st until band, when slightly stretched, fits up right front opening edge to neck shaping, ending with a WS row and with the addition of 5 buttonholes worked as foll:

Buttonhole row (RS): K3, K2tog, yo (to make a buttonhole), K2.

When band is complete, do NOT break off yarn.

Slip stitch band in place.

Collar

With RS facing, using size 6 (4mm) needles and yarn A, K 7 from right front band, pick up and knit 22 (23: 23: 23: 25: 25) sts up right side of neck, 31 (33: 33: 33: 35: 35) sts from back, and 22 (23: 23: 23: 25: 25) sts down left side of neck, then K 7 from left front band. 89 (93: 93: 93: 99: 99) sts.

Work in garter st for 3 rows, ending with a WS row.

Next row (RS of body): K3, K2tog, yo (to make 6th buttonhole), K to end.

Work in garter st for a further 4 rows.

Bind off 3 sts at beg of next 2 rows. 83 (87: 87: 87: 93: 93) sts.

Cont in garter st until collar measures 4¾in/12cm from pick-up row.

Bind off.

Front trim (make 4)

Cast on 321 (332: 332: 343: 343: 354) sts using size 3 (3mm) needles and yarn B.

**Row 1 (WS): Purl.

Row 2: K2, *K1 and slip this st back onto left needle, lift the next 8 sts on left needle over this st and off left needle, (yo) twice, K st on left needle again, K2, rep from * to end.

Row 3: K1, *P2tog, (K1, K1 tbl) into double yo of previous row, P1, rep from * to last st, K1. 118 (122: 122: 126: 126: 130) sts.

Row 4: Knit.

Bind off knitwise.**

Using photograph as a guide, sew bound-off edge of trims to fronts along P st lines near front bands.

Cuff trims (both alike)

Cast on 145 (145: 145: 156: 156: 156) sts using size 3 (3mm) needles and yarn B.

Work as given for front trim from ** to **, noting that there will be 54 (54: 54: 58: 58: 58) sts after row 3.

Sew bound-off edge of trims to cast-on edge of sleeves.

Collar trim

Cast on 343 (354: 354: 354: 376: 376) sts using size 3 (3mm) needles and yarn B.

Work as given for front trim from ** to **, noting that there will be 126 (130: 130: 130: 138: 138) sts after row 3.

Sew bound-off edge of trim to outer edge of collar as in photograph.

See page 124 for finishing instructions, setting in sleeves using the set-in method and leaving side seams open for first 34 rows.

BEADED TOP

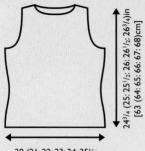

20 (21: 22: 23: 24: 25)in
[50.5 (53: 55.5: 58: 60.5: 63)cm]

24¾ (25: 25½: 26: 26½: 26¾)in
[63 (64: 65: 66: 67: 68)cm]

SIZES

1	2	3	4	5	6

TO FIT BUST

36	38	40	42	44	46	in
91	97	102	107	112	117	cm

YARN

Rowan 4 ply Soft—pale blue (370)

7	7	8	8	8	9 x 50g

NEEDLES

1 pair size 2 (2¾mm) needles
1 pair size 3 (3¼mm) needles

BEADS—approx 1,700 (1,800: 1,800: 1,900: 1,900: 2,000) 2.5mm clear glass beads (Rowan J3000-01007)

GAUGE

28 sts and 36 rows to 4in/10cm measured over St st using size 3 (3¼mm) needles.

SPECIAL ABBREVIATION

bead 1 = place a bead by bringing yarn to RS of work and slipping bead up next to st just worked, slip next st purlwise from left needle to right needle and take yarn to WS of work, leaving bead sitting on RS of work in front of slipped st. Do not place beads on edge stitches of work as this will interfere with seams.

Pattern note: Before starting to knit, thread beads onto yarn. To do this, thread a fine sewing needle (one that will easily pass through the beads) with sewing thread. Knot ends of thread and then pass end of yarn through this loop. Thread a bead onto sewing thread and then gently slide it along and onto knitting yarn. Continue in this way until required number of beads are on yarn.

BACK

Cast on 142 (150: 154: 162: 170: 178) sts using size 2 (2¾mm) needles.
Row 1 (RS): K2, *P2, K2, rep from * to end.

Row 2: P2, *K2, P2, rep from * to end.
These 2 rows form rib.
Work in rib for a further 4 rows, dec (dec: inc: inc: dec: dec) 1 st at center of last row and ending with a WS row. 141 (149: 155: 163: 169: 177) sts.
Change to size 3 (3¼mm) needles.
Beg and ending rows as indicated, working chart rows 1 to 18 once only and then rep rows 19 to 34 throughout, cont in patt from chart as foll:
Work 36 rows, ending with a WS row.
Dec 1 st at each end of next and every foll 10th row to 133 (141: 147: 155: 161: 169) sts, then on every foll 8th row until 129 (137: 143: 151: 157: 165) sts rem.
Work 11 rows, ending with a WS row.
Inc 1 st at each end of next and every foll 8th row until there are 141 (149: 155: 163: 169: 177) sts, taking inc sts into patt.
Work even until back measures 16½ (16¾: 16¾: 17¼: 17½: 17¾)in/42 (43: 43: 44: 44: 45)cm, ending with a WS row.
Shape armholes
Keeping patt correct, bind off 7 (8: 8: 9: 9: 10) sts at beg of next 2 rows. 127 (133: 139: 145: 151: 157) sts.
Dec 1 st at each end of next 9 (9: 11: 11: 13: 13) rows, then on foll 7 (8: 8: 9: 9: 10) alt rows, then on foll 4th row. 93 (97: 99: 103: 105: 109) sts.
Work even until armhole measures 8¼ (8¼: 8¾: 8¾: 9: 9)in/21 (21: 22: 22: 23: 23)cm, ending with a WS row.
Shape shoulders and back neck
Bind off 6 (7: 7: 8: 8: 8) sts at beg of next 2 rows. 81 (83: 85: 87: 89: 93) sts.
Next row (RS): Bind off 6 (7: 7: 8: 8: 8) sts, patt until there are 11 (10: 11: 11: 11: 13) sts on right needle and turn, leaving rem sts on a holder.
Work each side of neck separately.
Bind off 4 sts at beg of next row.
Bind off rem 7 (6: 7: 7: 7: 9) sts.
With RS facing, rejoin yarn to rem sts, bind off center 47 (49: 49: 49: 51: 51) sts, patt to end.

Complete to match first side, reversing shapings.

FRONT

Work as given for back until 24 (26: 26: 26: 26: 26) rows less have been worked than on back to start of shoulder shaping, ending with a WS row.

Shape neck

Next row (RS): Patt 32 (34: 35: 37: 37: 39) sts and turn, leaving rem sts on a holder. Work each side of neck separately.

Dec 1 st at neck edge of next 9 rows, then on foll 1 (2: 2: 2: 2: 2) alt rows, then on every foll 4th row until 19 (20: 21: 23: 23: 25) sts rem, ending with a WS row.

Shape shoulder

Bind off 6 (7: 7: 8: 8: 8) sts at beg of next and foll alt row.

Work 1 row.

Bind off rem 7 (6: 7: 7: 7: 9) sts.

With RS facing, rejoin yarn to rem sts, bind off center 29 (29: 29: 29: 31: 31) sts, patt to end.

Complete to match first side, reversing shapings.

FINISHING

BLOCK as described on page 123.

Join right shoulder seam using backstitch, or mattress stitch if preferred.

Neckband

With RS facing and using size 2 (2¾mm) needles, pick up and knit 23 (24: 24: 24: 24: 24) sts down left side of neck, 29 (29: 29: 29: 31: 31) sts from front, 23 (24: 24: 24: 24: 24) sts up right side of neck, then 55 (57: 57: 57: 59: 59) sts from back. 130 (134: 134: 134: 138: 138) sts.

Beg with row 1, work in rib as given for back for 2¾in/7cm.

Bind off in rib.

Join left shoulder and neckband seam.

Armhole borders (both alike)

With RS facing and using size 2 (2¾mm) needles, pick up and knit 130 (134: 138: 142: 146: 150) sts all round armhole edge.

Beg with row 1, work in rib as given for back for 5 rows.

Bind off in rib.

See page 124 for finishing instructions.

Key   □ K on RS, P on WS   ▣ bead 1

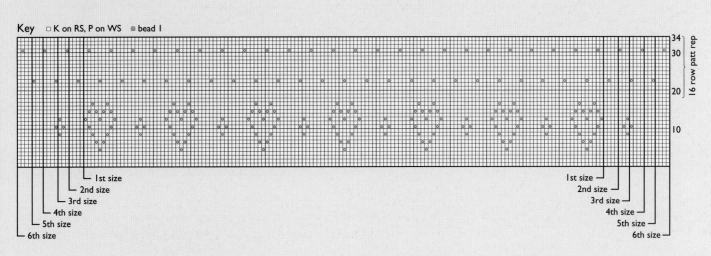

RUFFLED V-NECK SWEATER

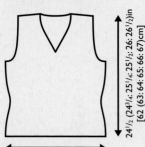

20 (21: 22: 23: 24: 25)in
[51 (53: 56: 58: 61: 63)cm]

24½ (24¾: 25¼: 25½: 26: 26½)in
[62 (63: 64: 65: 66: 67)cm]

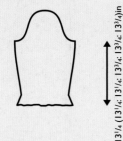

13¼ (13¼: 13¼: 13¾: 13¾: 13¾)in
[34 (34: 34: 35: 35: 35)cm]

SIZES

| 1 | 2 | 3 | 4 | 5 | 6 |

TO FIT BUST

| 36 | 38 | 40 | 42 | 44 | 46 | in |
| 91 | 97 | 102 | 107 | 112 | 117 | cm |

YARN

Rowan 4 ply Cotton—black (101) or chosen color

| 10 | 10 | 11 | 11 | 12 | 12 x 50g |

NEEDLES

1 pair size 1 (2¼mm) needles
1 pair size 3 (3mm) needles
Size 1 (2¼mm) circular needle

GAUGE

28 sts and 38 rows to 4in/10cm measured over St st using size 3 (3mm) needles.

BACK

Cast on 143 (149: 157: 163: 171: 177) sts using size 1 (2¼mm) needles.
Row 1 (RS): K1 (0: 2: 0: 0: 0), P3 (1: 3: 2: 0: 3), *K3, P3, rep from * to last 1 (4: 2: 5: 3: 0) sts, K1 (3: 2: 3: 3: 0), P0 (1: 0: 2: 0: 0).
Row 2: P1 (0: 2: 0: 0: 0), K3 (1: 3: 2: 0: 3), *P3, K3, rep from * to last 1 (4: 2: 5: 3: 0) sts, P1 (3: 2: 3: 3: 0), K0 (1: 0: 2: 0: 0).
These 2 rows form rib.
Cont in rib for a further 6 rows, ending with a WS row.
Change to size 3 (3mm) needles.
Beg with a K row, cont in St st, dec 1 st at each end of 29th (33rd: 33rd: 35th: 35th: 37th) and every foll 12th row to 137 (143: 151: 157: 165: 171) sts, then on every foll 10th row to 133 (139: 147: 153: 161: 167) sts, then on foll 8th row. 131 (137: 145: 151: 159: 165) sts.
Work 9 rows, ending with a WS row.
Inc 1 st at each end of next and every foll 8th row until there are 143 (149: 157: 163: 171: 177) sts.
Work even until back measures 15½ (15¾: 15¾: 16: 16¼: 16¾)in/39 (40: 40: 41: 41: 42)cm, ending with a WS row.

Shape armholes

Bind off 6 (7: 7: 8: 8: 9) sts at beg of next 2 rows. 131 (135: 143: 147: 155: 159) sts.**
Next row (RS): K3, K2tog, K to last 5 sts, K2tog tbl, K3.
Next row: P3, P2tog tbl, P to last 5 sts, P2tog, P3.
Working all decreases as set by last 2 rows, dec 1 st at each end of next 3 (3: 5: 5: 7: 7) rows, then on foll 4 (5: 5: 6: 6: 7) alt rows, then on every foll 4th row until 109 (111: 115: 117: 121: 123) sts rem.
Work even until armhole measures 9 (9: 9½: 9½: 9¾: 9¾)in/23 (23: 24: 24: 25: 25)cm, ending with a WS row.

Shape shoulders and back neck

Bind off 11 (11: 12: 12: 12: 13) sts at beg of next 2 rows. 87 (89: 91: 93: 97: 97) sts.
Next row (RS): Bind off 11 (11: 12: 12: 12: 13) sts, K until there are 15 (15: 15: 16: 17: 16) sts on right needle and turn, leaving rem sts on a holder.
Work each side of neck separately.
Bind off 4 sts at beg of next row.
Bind off rem 11 (11: 11: 12: 13: 12) sts.
With RS facing, rejoin yarn to rem sts, bind off center 35 (37: 37: 37: 39: 39) sts, K to end.
Complete to match first side, reversing shapings.

FRONT

Work as given for back to **.
Working all armhole decreases as set by back, dec 1 st at each end of next 5 (5: 7: 7: 9: 9) rows, then on foll 4 (5: 5: 5: 4: 4) alt rows, then on foll 4th (0: 0: 0: 0: 0) row. 111 (115: 119: 123: 129: 133) sts.
Work 1 (3: 1: 1: 1: 1) rows, ending with a WS row.

Divide for neck

Next row (RS): (K3, K2tog) 0 (1: 0: 1: 1: 1) times, K55 (52: 59: 56: 59: 61) and turn, leaving rem sts on a holder. 55 (56: 59: 60: 63: 65) sts.
Work each side of neck separately.
Dec 1 st at armhole edge of 2nd (4th: 2nd: 4th: 2nd: 2nd) and foll 0(0: 0: 0: 0: 1) alt row, then

on 0 (0: 1: 1: 2: 2) foll 4th rows **and at same time** dec 1 st at neck edge on 2nd and every foll alt row. 53 (53: 54: 54: 55: 55) sts.

Dec 1 st at neck edge **only** on 2nd and foll 12 (13: 10: 9: 8: 7) alt rows, then on every foll 4th row until 33 (33: 35: 36: 37: 38) sts rem.

Work even until front matches back to start of shoulder shaping, ending with a WS row.

Shape shoulder
Bind off 11 (11: 12: 12: 12: 13) sts at beg of next and foll alt row.

Work 1 row.

Bind off rem 11 (11: 11: 12: 13: 12) sts.

With RS facing, rejoin yarn to rem sts, K2tog, K to last 0 (5: 0: 5: 5: 5) sts, (K2tog tbl, K3) 0 (1: 0: 1: 1: 1) times. 55 (56: 59: 60: 63: 65) sts.

Complete to match first side, reversing shapings.

SLEEVES (both alike)
Cast on 63 (65: 65: 67: 69: 69) sts using size 3 (3mm) needles.

Beg with a K row, cont in St st, shaping sides by inc 1 st at each end of 5th and every foll 4th row to 67 (69: 81: 79: 87: 93) sts, then on every foll 6th row until there are 95 (97: 101: 103: 107: 109) sts.

Work even until sleeve measures 11¼ (11¼: 11¼: 11¾: 11¾: 11¾)in/29 (29: 29: 30: 30: 30)cm, ending with a WS row.

Shape sleeve cap
Bind off 6 (7: 7: 8: 8: 9) sts at beg of next 2 rows. 83 (83: 87: 87: 91: 91) sts.

Working all decreases as set by armholes, dec 1 st at each end of next 7 rows, then on foll 5 alt rows, then on every foll 4th row until 45 (45: 49: 49: 53: 53) sts rem.

Work 1 row, ending with a WS row.

Dec 1 st at each end of next and every foll alt row to 39 sts, then on foll 5 rows, ending with a WS row.

Bind off rem 29 sts.

FINISHING
BLOCK as described on page 123.
Join both shoulder seams using backstitch.

Neck ruffle
Cast on 163 (169: 169: 169: 175: 175) sts using size 1 (2¼mm) circular needle.

***Row 1 (WS): K3, *P1, K5, rep from * to last 4 sts, P1, K3.

Row 2: P3, *yo, K1, yo, P5, rep from * to last 4 sts, yo, K1, yo, P3.

Row 3: K3, *P3, K5, rep from * to last 6 sts, P3, K3.

Row 4: P3, *yo, K3, yo, P5, rep from * to last 6 sts, yo, K3, yo, P3.

Row 5: K3, *P5, K5, rep from * to last 8 sts, P5, K3.

Row 6: P3, *yo, K5, yo, P5, rep from * to last 8 sts, yo, K5, yo, P3.

Row 7: K3, *P7, K5, rep from * to last 10 sts, P7, K3.

Row 8: P3, *yo, K7, yo, P5, rep from * to last 10 sts, yo, K7, yo, P3.

Row 9: K3, *P9, K5, rep from * to last 12 sts, P9, K3.

Row 10: P3, *yo, K9, yo, P5, rep from * to last 12 sts, yo, K9, yo, P3.

Row 11: K3, *P11, K5, rep from * to last 14 sts, P11, K3.

Row 12: P3, *yo, K11, yo, P5, rep from * to last 14 sts, yo, K11, yo, P3.

Row 13: K3, *P13, K5, rep from * to last 16 sts, P13, K3.

Row 14: P3, *yo, K13, yo, P5, rep from * to last 16 sts, yo, K13, yo, P3.

Row 15: K3, *P15, K5, rep from * to last 18 sts, P15, K3.

Row 16: P3, *yo, K15, yo, P5, rep from * to last 18 sts, yo, K15, yo, P3.

Row 17: K3, *P17, K5, rep from * to last 20 sts, P17, K3.

Row 18: P3, *yo, K17, yo, P5, rep from * to last 20 sts, yo, K17, yo, P3.

Row 19: K3, *P19, K5, rep from * to last 22 sts, P19, K3.

Row 20: P3, *yo, K19, yo, P5, rep from * to last 22 sts, yo, K19, yo, P3. 703 (729: 729: 729: 755: 755) sts.

Row 21: K3, *P21, K5, rep from * to last 24 sts, P21, K3.

Work picot bind-off as foll: *cast on 2 sts, bind off 5 sts, slip st on right needle back onto left needle, rep from * until all sts are bound off.***

Join row-end edges of neck ruffle, then sew cast-on edge to neck edge, positioning seam at center back neck.

Cuff ruffles (both alike)
Cast on 67 (67: 73: 73: 73: 73) sts using size 1 (2¼mm) circular needle.

Work as given for neck ruffle from *** to ***, noting that there will be 287 (287: 313: 313: 313: 313) sts after row 20.

Sew cast-on edge of cuff ruffles to cast-on edge of sleeves.

See page 124 for finishing instructions, setting in sleeves using the set-in method.

FLOWER-TRIM JACKET

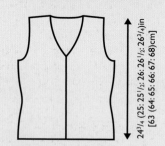

20¹/₂ (21¹/₂: 22¹/₂: 23¹/₂: 24¹/₂: 25¹/₂)in
[51.5 (54: 57: 59.5: 62.5: 65)cm]

24³/₄ (25: 25¹/₂: 26: 26¹/₂: 26³/₄)in
[63 (64: 65: 66: 67: 68)cm]

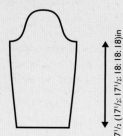

7¹/₂ (17¹/₂: 17¹/₂: 18: 18: 18)in
[45 (45: 45: 46: 46: 46)cm]

SIZES

1	2	3	4	5	6

TO FIT BUST

36	38	40	42	44	46	in
91	97	102	107	112	117	cm

YARNS

Jaeger Extra Fine Merino DK
A charcoal (959)

13	13	14	15	15	16 x 50g

Rowan Kidsilk Haze
B dark gray (605)

1	1	1	1	1	1 x 25g

NEEDLES

1 pair size 3 (3mm) needles
1 pair size 5 (3¾mm) needles

BUTTONS—6

BEADS—approx 420 2.5mm metallic gray beads (Rowan J3000-01006)

GAUGE

22 sts and 30 rows to 4in/10cm measured over St st using size 5 (3¾mm) needles and yarn A.

SPECIAL ABBREVIATIONS

make loop = insert right needle into next st and take yarn around right needle point as though to K this st, wrap yarn around one finger of left hand then over right needle point again (2 loops on right needle point), draw both these loops through st on left needle slipping st off left needle, insert left needle point into front of both these loops now on right needle and K them tog tbl.

make beaded loop = insert right needle into next st and take yarn around right needle point as though to K this st, slide bead along yarn leaving it approx ¾in/2cm from right needle point, wrap yarn around one finger of left hand then over right needle point again (2 loops on right needle point) ensuring bead is

on this loop, draw both these loops through st on left needle slipping st off left needle, insert left needle point into front of both these loops now on right needle and K them tog tbl.

BACK

Cast on 113 (119: 125: 131: 137: 143) sts using size 3 (3mm) needles and yarn A.
Row 1 (RS): K1, *P1, K1, rep from * to end.
Row 2: Rep row 1.
These 2 rows form seed st.
Work in seed st for a further 8 rows, ending with a WS row.
Change to size 5 (3¾mm) needles.
Beg with a K row, cont in St st, dec 1 st at each end of 27th (29th: 29th: 29th: 29th: 29th) and every foll 10th row to 107 (113: 119: 125: 131: 137) sts, then on every foll 8th row until there are 103 (109: 115: 121: 127: 133) sts.
Work 7 rows, ending with a WS row.
Inc 1 st at each end of next and every foll 8th row until there are 113 (119: 125: 131: 137: 143) sts.
Work even until back measures 15¾ (16: 16: 16½: 16¾: 17)in/40 (41: 41: 42: 42: 43)cm, ending with a WS row.
Shape armholes
Bind off 5 (6: 6: 7: 7: 8) sts at beg of next 2 rows. 103 (107: 113: 117: 123: 127) sts.
Next row (RS): K3, K2tog, K to last 5 sts, K2tog tbl, K3.
Next row: P3, P2tog tbl, P to last 5 sts, P2tog, P3.
Working all armhole decreases as set by last 2 rows, dec 1 st at each end of next 1 (1: 3: 3: 5: 5) rows, then on foll 3 (4: 4: 5: 5: 6) alt rows, then on every foll 4th row until 87 (89: 91: 93: 95: 97) sts rem.
Work even until armhole measures 9 (9: 9½: 9½: 9¾: 9¾)in/23 (23: 24: 24: 25: 25)cm, ending with a WS row.
Shape shoulders and back neck
Bind off 9 (9: 9: 9: 9: 10) sts at beg of next 2 rows. 69 (71: 73: 75: 77: 77) sts.
Next row (RS): Bind off 9 (9: 9: 9: 9: 10) sts, K until there are 12 (12: 13: 14: 14: 13) sts on

right needle and turn, leaving rem sts on a holder.

Work each side of neck separately.

Bind off 4 sts at beg of next row.

Bind off rem 8 (8: 9: 10: 10: 9) sts.

With RS facing, rejoin yarn to rem sts, bind off center 27 (29: 29: 29: 31: 31) sts, K to end.

Complete to match first side, reversing shapings.

LEFT FRONT

Cast on 63 (67: 69: 73: 75: 79) sts using size 3 (3mm) needles and yarn A.

Work in seed st as given for back for 9 rows, ending with a RS row.

Row 10 (WS): Seed st 7 sts and slip these onto a holder, seed st to last 1 (0: 1: 0: 1: 0) st, (inc in last st) 1 (0: 1: 0: 1: 0) times. 57 (60: 63: 66: 69: 72) sts.

Change to size 5 (3¾mm) needles.

Beg with a K row, cont in St st, dec 1 st at beg of 27th (29th: 29th: 29th: 29th: 29th) and every foll 10th row to 54 (57: 60: 63: 66: 69) sts, then on every foll 8th row until there are 52 (55: 58: 61: 64: 67) sts.

Work 7 rows, ending with a WS row.

Inc 1 st at beg of next and every foll 8th row until there are 57 (60: 63: 66: 69: 72) sts.

Work even until left front matches back to beg of armhole shaping, ending with a WS row.

Shape armhole

Bind off 5 (6: 6: 7: 7: 8) sts at beg of next row. 52 (54: 57: 59: 62: 64) sts.

Work 1 row.

Working all armhole decreases as set by back, dec 1 st at armhole edge of next 3 (3: 4: 4: 4: 4) rows. 49 (51: 53: 55: 58: 60) sts.

Work 1 (1: 0: 0: 0: 0) row, ending with a WS row.

Shape front slope

Working all front slope decreases in same way as armhole decreases, dec 1 st at armhole edge of next 1 (1: 1: 1: 3: 3) rows, then on foll 2 (3: 4: 5: 5: 6) alt rows, then on 2 foll 4th rows **and at same time** dec 1 st at front slope edge of next and foll 6 (7: 8: 8: 8: 8) alt

rows, then on foll 0 (0: 0: 0: 4th: 4th) row. 37 (37: 37: 38: 38: 39) sts.

Dec 1 st at front slope edge only on 2nd (2nd: 4th: 2nd: 4th: 2nd) and foll 0 (1: 0: 0: 0: 0) alt rows, then on every foll 4th row until 26 (26: 27: 28: 28: 29) sts rem.

Work even until left front matches back to start of shoulder shaping, ending with a WS row.

Shape shoulder

Bind off 9 (9: 9: 9: 9: 10) sts at beg of next and foll alt row.

Work 1 row.

Bind off rem 8 (8: 9: 10: 10: 9) sts.

RIGHT FRONT

Cast on 63 (67: 69: 73: 75: 79) sts using size 3 (3mm) needles and yarn A.

Work in seed st as given for back for 4 rows, ending with a WS row.

Row 5 (RS): Seed st 3 sts, work 2 tog, yo (to make first buttonhole), seed st to end.

Work in seed st for a further 4 rows, ending with a RS row.

Row 10 (WS): (Inc in first st) 1 (0: 1: 0: 1: 0) times, seed st to last 7 sts and turn, leaving rem 7 sts on a holder. 57 (60: 63: 66: 69: 72) sts.

Change to size 5 (3¾mm) needles.

Beg with a K row, cont in St st, dec 1 st at end of 27th (29th: 29th: 29th: 29th: 29th) and every foll 10th row to 54 (57: 60: 63: 66: 69) sts, then on every foll 8th row until there are 52 (55: 58: 61: 64: 67) sts.

Complete to match left front, reversing shapings.

SLEEVES (both alike)

Cast on 57 (59: 59: 61: 63: 63) sts using size 3 (3mm) needles and yarn A.

Row 1 (RS): P0 (1: 1: 2: 3: 3), *K3, P3, rep from * to last 3 (4: 4: 5: 6: 6) sts, K3, P0 (1: 1: 2: 3: 3).

Row 2: K0 (1: 1: 2: 3: 3), *P3, K3, rep from * to last 3 (4: 4: 5: 6: 6) sts, P3, K0 (1: 1: 2: 3: 3).

These 2 rows form rib.

Cont in rib for a further 18 rows, ending with a WS row.

Change to size 5 (3¾mm) needles.

Beg with a K row, cont in St st, inc 1 st at each end of next and every foll 8th row to 69 (71: 81: 79: 81: 91) sts, then on every foll 10th (10th: 10th: 10th: 10th: -) row until there are 81 (83: 85: 87: 89: -) sts.

Work even until sleeve measures 17½ (17½: 17½: 18: 18: 18)in/45 (45: 45: 46: 46: 46)cm, ending with a WS row.

Shape sleeve cap

Bind off 5 (6: 6: 7: 7: 8) sts at beg of next 2 rows. 71 (71: 73: 73: 75: 75) sts.

Working all decreases as set by back and front armholes, dec 1 st at each end of next 5 rows, then on foll 4 alt rows, then on every foll 4th row until 45 (45: 47: 47: 49: 49) sts rem.

Work 1 row, ending with a WS row.

Dec 1 st at each end of next and every foll alt row to 37 sts, then on foll 7 rows, ending with a WS row. Bind off rem 23 sts.

FINISHING

BLOCK as described on page 123.

Join both shoulder seams using backstitch, or mattress stitch if preferred.

Left front band

Slip 7 sts from left front holder onto size 3 (3mm) needles and rejoin yarn A with RS facing.

Cont in seed st until band, when slightly stretched, fits up left front opening edge, up left front slope and across to center back neck, ending with a WS row.

Bind off in seed st.

Slip stitch band in place.

Mark positions for 6 buttons on this band— first to come level with buttonhole already worked in right front, last to come ½in/1cm below start of front slope shaping, and rem 4 buttons evenly spaced between.

Right front band

Slip 7 sts from right front holder onto size 3 (3mm) needles and rejoin yarn A with WS facing.

Cont in seed st until band, when slightly stretched, fits up right front opening edge, up right front slope and across to center back neck, ending with a WS row and with the addition of a further 5 buttonholes worked as foll:

Buttonhole row (RS): Seed st 3 sts, work 2 tog, yo (to make first buttonhole), seed st 2 sts.

When band is complete, bind off in seed st. Slip stitch band in place, joining ends of bands at center back neck.

Flowers (make 13)

Flowers are worked using yarn B DOUBLE throughout. Before starting, thread 26 beads onto yarn B for each flower.

Cast on 41 sts using size 5 (3¾mm) needles and yarn B DOUBLE.

Row 1 (WS): K1, *make loop, K1, make beaded loop, K1, rep from * to end.

Row 2: Knit.

Row 3: K2, *make loop, K1, make beaded loop, K1, rep from * to last 3 sts, make loop, K2.

Row 4: (K2, K2tog) 10 times, K1. 31 sts.

Row 5: K1, *make loop, K1, make beaded loop, K1, rep from * to last 2 sts, make loop, K1.

Row 6: K1, (K2tog) 14 times, K2. 17 sts.

Row 7: Rep row 1.

Row 8: K1, (K2tog) 7 times, K2. 10 sts.

Row 9: (K2tog) 5 times.

Break yarn and thread through rem 5 sts. Pull up tight and fasten off securely.

Join row-ends of flower, then sew flowers to neck edge of garment as in photograph by attaching 5 or 6 beads at center.

See page 124 for finishing instructions, setting in sleeves using the set-in method.

POODLE-COLLAR JACKET

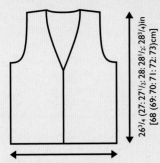

26¾ (27: 27½: 28: 28½: 28¾)in
[68 (69: 70: 71: 72: 73)cm]

22½ (23½: 24½: 25½: 26½: 28)in
[57 (60: 62: 65.5: 67.5: 70.5)cm]

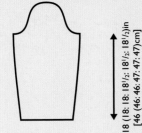

18 (18: 18: 18½: 18½: 18½)in
[46 (46: 46: 47: 47: 47)cm]

SIZES

1	2	3	4	5	6

TO FIT BUST

36	38	40	42	44	46	in
91	97	102	107	112	117	cm

YARN

Rowan Kid Classic—light aqua (822)

11	11	12	12	13	13 × 50g

NEEDLES

1 pair size 6 (4mm) needles
1 pair size 7 (4½mm) needles
1 pair of size 8 (5mm) needles

BUTTONS—4

GAUGE

19 sts and 25 rows to 4in/10cm measured over St st using size 8 (5mm) needles.

SPECIAL ABBREVIATIONS

make loop = K1 leaving st on left needle, bring yarn to front of work between needles and wrap it twice round thumb of left hand, take yarn back to WS of work between needles and K same st again, letting st slip off left needle, bring yarn to front of work between needles and take it back to WS over right needle point, lift last 2 sts on right needle over this loop and off right needle.

BACK

Cast on 108 (114: 118: 124: 128: 134) sts using size 6 (4mm) needles.
Row 1 (RS): K1 (0: 0: 1: 0: 0), P2 (2: 0: 2: 1: 0), *K2, P2, rep from * to last 1 (0: 2: 1: 3: 2) sts, K1 (0: 2: 1: 2: 2), P0 (0: 0: 0: 1: 0).
Row 2: P1 (0: 0: 1: 0: 0), K2 (2: 0: 2: 1: 0), *P2, K2, rep from * to last 1 (0: 2: 1: 3: 2) sts, P1 (0: 2: 1: 2: 2), K0 (0: 0: 0: 1: 0).
These 2 rows form rib.
Cont in rib for a further 16 rows, ending with a WS row.
Change to size 8 (5mm) needles.

Beg with a K row, cont in St st until back measures 17¾ (18: 18: 18½: 18¾: 19)in/45 (46: 46: 47: 47: 48)cm, ending with a WS row.
Shape armholes
Bind off 5 (6: 6: 7: 7: 8) sts at beg of next 2 rows. 98 (102: 106: 110: 114: 118) sts.
Next row (RS): K3, K2tog, K to last 5 sts, K2tog tbl, K3.
Next row: P3, P2tog tbl, P to last 5 sts, P2tog, P3.
Working all decreases as set by last 2 rows, dec 1 st at each end of next 3 (3: 5: 5: 7: 7) rows, then on foll 5 (6: 5: 6: 5: 6) alt rows, then on every foll 4th row until 74 (76: 78: 80: 82: 84) sts rem.
Work even until armhole measures 9 (9: 9½: 9½: 9¾: 9¾)in/23 (23: 24: 24: 25: 25)cm, ending with a WS row.
Shape shoulders and back neck
Bind off 7 (7: 8: 8: 8: 8) sts at beg of next 2 rows. 60 (62: 62: 64: 66: 68) sts.
Next row (RS): Bind off 7 (7: 8: 8: 8: 8) sts, K until there are 12 (12: 11: 12: 12: 13) sts on right needle and turn, leaving rem sts on a holder.
Work each side of neck separately.
Bind off 4 sts at beg of next row.
Bind off rem 8 (8: 7: 8: 8: 9) sts.
With RS facing, rejoin yarn to rem sts, bind off center 22 (24: 24: 24: 26: 26) sts, K to end.
Complete to match first side, reversing shapings.

LEFT FRONT

Cast on 69 (72: 74: 77: 79: 82) sts using size 6 (4mm) needles.
Row 1 (RS): K1 (0: 0: 1: 0: 0), P2 (2: 0: 2: 1: 0), *K2, P2, rep from * to last 2 sts, K2.
Row 2: *P2, K2, rep from * to last 1 (0: 2: 1: 3: 2) sts, P1 (0: 2: 1: 2: 2), K0 (0: 0: 0: 1: 0).
These 2 rows form rib.
Cont in rib for a further 15 rows, ending with a RS row.
Row 18 (WS): Rib 14 and slip these sts onto a holder, rib to end. 55 (58: 60: 63: 65: 68) sts.

Change to size 8 (5mm) needles.
Beg with a K row, cont in St st until 18 rows less have been worked than on back to beg of armhole shaping, ending with a WS row.

Shape front slope

Dec 1 st at end of next and every foll 4th row until 50 (53: 55: 58: 60: 63) sts rem.
Work 1 row, ending with a WS row. (Left front should now match back to beg of armhole shaping.)

Shape armhole

Bind off 5 (6: 6: 7: 7: 8) sts at beg of next row. 45 (47: 49: 51: 53: 55) sts.
Work 1 row.
Working all armhole decreases as set by back, dec 1 st at armhole edge of next 5 (5: 7: 7: 9: 9) rows, then on foll 5 (6: 5: 6: 5: 6) alt rows, then on 2 foll 4th rows **and at same time** dec 1 st at front slope edge of next and every foll 4th row. 27 (27: 28: 29: 30: 30) sts.
Dec 1 st at front slope edge only on 2nd (4th: 4th: 2nd: 2nd: 4th) and every foll 6th (4th: 4th: 4th: 4th: 4th) row to 22 (24: 26: 27: 26: 27) sts, then on every foll - (6th: 6th: 6th: 6th: 6th) row until - (22: 23: 24: 24: 25) sts rem.
Work even until left front matches back to start of shoulder shaping, ending with a WS row.

Shape shoulder

Bind off 7 (7: 8: 8: 8: 8) sts at beg of next and foll alt row.
Work 1 row.
Bind off rem 8 (8: 7: 8: 8: 9) sts.

RIGHT FRONT

Cast on 69 (72: 74: 77: 79: 82) sts using size 6 (4mm) needles.
Row 1 (RS): *K2, P2, rep from * to last 1 (0: 2: 1: 3: 2) sts, K1 (0: 2: 1: 2: 2), P0 (0: 0: 0: 1: 0).
Row 2: P1 (0: 0: 1: 0: 0), K2 (2: 0: 2: 1: 0), *P2, K2, rep from * to last 2 sts, P2.
These 2 rows form rib.
Cont in rib for a further 6 rows, ending with a WS row.
Row 9 (buttonhole row) (RS): Rib 4, bind off 4 sts (to make a buttonhole—cast on 4 sts

over these bound-off sts on next row), rib to end.
Cont in rib for a further 8 rows, ending with a RS row.
Row 18 (WS): Rib to last 14 sts and turn, leaving rem 14 sts on a holder. 55 (58: 60: 63: 65: 68) sts.
Change to size 8 (5mm) needles.
Beg with a K row, cont in St st until 18 rows less have been worked than on back to beg of armhole shaping, ending with a WS row.

Shape front slope

Dec 1 st at beg of next and every foll 4th row until 50 (53: 55: 58: 60: 63) sts rem.
Complete to match left front, reversing shapings.

SLEEVES (both alike)

Cast on 44 (46: 46: 48: 50: 50) sts using size 6 (4mm) needles.
Row 1 (RS): P1 (0: 0: 1: 0: 0), *K2, P2, rep from * to last 3 (2: 2: 3: 2: 2) sts, K2, P1 (0: 0: 1: 0: 0).
Row 2: K1 (0: 0: 1: 0: 0), *P2, K2, rep from * to last 3 (2: 2: 3: 2: 2) sts, P2, K1 (0: 0: 1: 0: 0).
These 2 rows form rib.
Cont in rib for a further 16 rows, ending with a WS row.
Change to size 8 (5mm) needles.
Beg with a K row, cont in St st, shaping sides by inc 1 st at each end of next and every foll 6th (6th: 6th: 6th: 6th: 4th) row to 66 (68: 76: 74: 76: 54) sts, then on every foll 8th (8th: -: 8th: 8th: 6th) row until there are 72 (74: -: 78: 80: 82) sts.
Work even until sleeve measures 18 (18: 18: 18½: 18½: 18½)in/46 (46: 46: 47: 47: 47)cm, ending with a WS row.

Shape sleeve cap

Bind off 5 (6: 6: 7: 7: 8) sts at beg of next 2 rows. 62 (62: 64: 64: 66: 66) sts.
Working all decreases as set by armholes, dec 1 st at each end of next 7 rows, then on foll 5 alt rows, then on every foll 4th row until 34 (34: 36: 36: 38: 38) sts rem.
Work 1 row, ending with a WS row.

Dec 1 st at each end of next and every foll alt row to 26 sts, then on foll 3 rows, ending with a WS row.
Bind off rem 20 sts.

FINISHING

BLOCK as described on page 123.
Join both shoulder seams using backstitch, or mattress stitch if preferred.

Left front band

Slip 14 sts from left front holder onto size 6 (4mm) needles and rejoin yarn with RS facing.
Cont in rib as set until band, when slightly stretched, fits up left front opening edge to start of front slope shaping, ending with a WS row.
Bind off in rib.
Slip stitch band in place.
Mark positions for 4 buttons on this band—first to come level with buttonhole already worked in right front, last to come ½in/1cm below start of front slope shaping, and rem 2 buttons evenly spaced between.

Right front band

Slip 14 sts from right front holder onto size 6 (4mm) needles and rejoin yarn with WS facing.
Cont in rib as set until band, when slightly stretched, fits up right front opening edge to start of front slope shaping, ending with a WS row and with the addition of a further 3 buttonholes to correspond with positions marked for buttons worked as foll:
Buttonhole row (RS): Rib 4, bind off 4 sts (to make a buttonhole—cast on 4 sts over these bound-off sts on next row), rib to end.
When band is complete, bind off in rib.
Slip stitch band in place.

Collar

Cast on 7 sts using size 7 (4½mm) needles.
Row 1 (WS): Knit.
Row 2: Inc in first st, *make loop, K1, rep from * to end. 8 sts.
Row 3: Knit.
Row 4: Inc in first st, *make loop, K1, rep from * to last st, K1. 9 sts.
Rows 5 to 8: Rep rows 1 to 4. 11 sts.

Row 9: K to last st, inc in last st. 12 sts.
Row 10: Inc in first st, K1, *make loop, K1, rep from * to end. 13 sts.
Row 11: Rep row 9. 14 sts.
Row 12: Rep row 4. 15 sts.
Rows 13 to 20: Rep rows 9 to 12, twice. 23 sts.
Rows 21 to 40: Rep rows 1 to 4, 5 times. 33 sts.
Row 41: Knit.
Row 42: K1, *make loop, K1, rep from * to end.
Row 43: Knit.
Row 44: K2, *make loop, K1, rep from * to last st, K1.
Last 4 rows form loop patt.
Cont in loop patt until collar measures 28¼ (29: 30: 30: 31½: 31½)in/72 (74: 76: 76: 80: 80)cm, ending with a RS row.
Keeping loop patt correct, dec 1 st at shaped edge of next and every foll alt row to 21 sts, then on foll 11 rows, then on foll 3 alt rows, ending with a RS row.
Bind off rem 7 sts.
Sew cast-on and bound-off ends of collar to top of front bands, and straight row-end edge of collar to front slope and back neck edges.
See page 124 for finishing instructions, setting in sleeves using the set-in method.

LACE-SLEEVE SWEATER

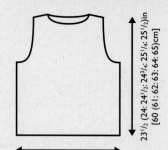

20³/₄ (21³/₄: 22³/₄: 23³/₄: 24³/₄: 25³/₄)in
[52.5 (55: 58: 60.5: 63: 65.5)cm]

23½ (24: 24½: 24³/₄: 25¹/₄: 25½)in
[60 (61: 62: 63: 64: 65)cm]

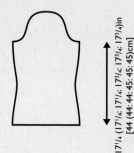

17¹/₄ (17¹/₄: 17¹/₄: 17³/₄: 17³/₄: 17³/₄)in
[44 (44: 44: 45: 45: 45)cm]

SIZES

1	2	3	4	5	6

TO FIT BUST

36	38	40	42	44	46	in
91	97	102	107	112	117	cm

YARN

Rowan Cotton Glace—black (727)

13	14	14	15	16	16 x 50g

NEEDLES

1 pair size 2 (2¾mm) needles
1 pair size 3 (3¼mm) needles
Size 2 (2¾mm) circular needle
2 double-pointed size 2 (2¾mm)
needles

GAUGE

23 sts and 32 rows to 4in/10cm measured over St st, 22 sts and 36 rows to 4in/10cm measured over lace pattern using size 3 (3¼mm) needles.

BACK

Cast on 121 (127: 133: 139: 145: 151) sts using size 2 (2¾mm) needles.
Work in garter st for 8 rows, ending with a WS row.
Change to size 3 (3¼mm) needles.
Row 5 (RS): Knit.
Row 6: K5, P to last 5 sts, K5.
Rep last 2 rows 12 times more, ending with a WS row.
Beg with a K row, cont in St st until back measures 14½ (15: 15: 15¼: 15½: 15¾)in/37 (38: 38: 39: 39: 40)cm from fold line row, ending with a WS row.
Shape armholes
Bind off 6 (7: 7: 8: 8: 9) sts at beg of next 2 rows. 109 (113: 119: 123: 129: 133) sts.
Dec 1 st at each end of next 5 (5: 7: 7: 9: 9) rows, then on foll 4 (5: 5: 6: 6: 7) alt rows, then on every foll 4th row until 87 (89: 91: 93: 95: 97) sts rem.
Work even until armhole measures 9 (9: 9½:

9½: 9¾: 9¾)in/23 (23: 24: 24: 25: 25)cm, ending with a WS row.
Shape shoulders and back neck
Bind off 6 (6: 6: 7: 7: 7) sts at beg of next 2 rows. 75 (77: 79: 79: 81: 83) sts.
Next row (RS): Bind off 6 (6: 6: 7: 7: 7) sts, K until there are 10 (10: 11: 10: 10: 11) sts on right needle and turn, leaving rem sts on a holder.
Work each side of neck separately.
Bind off 4 sts at beg of next row.
Bind off rem 6 (6: 7: 6: 6: 7) sts.
With RS facing, rejoin yarn to rem sts, bind off center 43 (45: 45: 45: 47: 47) sts, K to end.
Complete to match first side, reversing shapings.

FRONT

Work as given for back until 10 (12: 12: 12: 12: 12) rows less have been worked than on back to start of shoulder shaping, ending with a WS row.
Shape neck
Next row (RS): K32 (33: 34: 35: 35: 36) and turn, leaving rem sts on a holder.
Work each side of neck separately.
Bind off 5 sts at beg of next and foll alt row. 22 (23: 24: 25: 25: 26) sts.
Dec 1 st at neck edge of next 3 rows, then on foll 1 (2: 2: 2: 2: 2) alt rows. 18 (18: 19: 20: 20: 21) sts.
Work 1 row, ending with a WS row.
Shape shoulder
Bind off 6 (6: 6: 7: 7: 7) sts at beg of next and foll alt row.
Work 1 row.
Bind off rem 6 (6: 7: 6: 6: 7) sts.
With RS facing, rejoin yarn to rem sts, bind off center 23 (23: 23: 23: 25: 25) sts, K to end.
Complete to match first side, reversing shapings.

SLEEVES (both alike)

Cast on 85 (87: 87: 89: 91: 91) sts using size 2 (2¾mm) needles.
Beg with a K row, work in St st for 3 rows.

Row 4 (WS): Knit (to form fold line).
Beg with a K row, work in St st for 3 rows, ending with a RS row.
Row 8 (WS): P10, P2tog, *P19 (20: 20: 20: 21: 21), P2tog, rep from * twice more, P to end. 81 (83: 83: 85: 87: 87) sts.
Change to size 3 (3¼mm) needles.
Cont in lace patt as foll:
Row 1 (RS): K0 (1: 1: 2: 1: 1), (yo, skp) 0 (0: 0: 0: 1: 1) times, *K1, (K2tog, yo) twice, K1, (yo, skp) twice, rep from * to last 1 (2: 2: 3: 4: 4) sts, K1 (2: 2: 3: 1: 1), (K2tog, yo, K1) 0 (0: 0: 0: 1: 1) times.
Row 2: Purl.
Row 3: K0 (1: 1: 1: 2: 2), (yo, sl 1, K2tog, psso, yo) 0 (0: 0: 1: 1: 1) times, (K2tog, yo) 2 (2: 2: 1: 1: 1) times, K3, *yo, skp, yo, sl 1, K2tog, psso, yo, K2tog, yo, K3, rep from * to last 4 (5: 5: 6: 7: 7) sts, (yo, skp) 2 (2: 2: 1: 1: 1) times, (yo, sl 1, K2tog, psso, yo) 0 (0: 0: 1: 1: 1) times, K0 (1: 1: 1: 2: 2).
Row 4: Purl.
These 4 rows form lace patt.
Cont in lace patt, dec 1 st at each end of 5th and every foll 8th row to 71 (73: 73: 75: 77: 77) sts, then on every foll 10th row until 65 (67: 67: 69: 71: 71) sts rem.
Work 9 rows, ending with a WS row.
Inc 1 st at each end of next and every foll 8th (8th: 6th: 6th: 6th: 4th) row to 81 (83: 85: 83: 93: 79) sts, then on every foll - (-: 8th: 8th: -: 6th) row until there are - (-: 87: 89: -: 95) sts, taking inc sts into patt.
Work even until sleeve measures 17¼ (17¼: 17¼: 17¾: 17¾: 17¾)in/44 (44: 44: 45: 45: 45)cm from fold line row, ending with a WS row.
Shape sleeve cap
Keeping patt correct, bind off 6 (7: 7: 8: 8: 9) sts at beg of next 2 rows. 69 (69: 73: 73: 77: 77) sts.
Dec 1 st at each end of next 7 rows, then on foll alt row to 49 sts, then on every foll 4th row until 33 sts rem.
Work 1 row, ending with a WS row.
Dec 1 st at each end of next and foll alt row,

then on foll 3 rows, ending with a WS row. Bind off rem 23 sts.

FINISHING

BLOCK as described on page 123.
Join both shoulder seams using backstitch, or mattress stitch if preferred.
Place marker on center front neck st.
Neckband
With RS facing and using size 2 (2¾mm) circular needle, starting and ending at marked center front neck st, pick up and knit 11 (11: 11: 11: 12: 12) sts from right section of bound-off neck sts, 17 (19: 19: 19: 19: 19) sts up right side of neck, 50 (52: 52: 52: 54: 54) sts from back, 17 (19: 19: 19: 19: 19) sts down left side of neck, then 11 (11: 11: 11: 12: 12) sts from left section of bound-off neck sts. 106 (112: 112: 112: 116: 116) sts.
Working backward and forward in rows, not rounds, cont as foll:
Beg with a P row, work in St st for 3 rows.
Row 4 (RS): Purl (to form fold line).
Beg with a P row, work in St st for 3 rows, ending with a WS row.
Bind off.
Neck tie
With size 2 (2¾mm) double-pointed needles, cast on 3 sts.
Row 1 (RS): K3, *without turning work push, these 3 sts to opposite end of needle and bring yarn to opposite end of work, pulling it quite tightly across back of these 3 sts. Using other needle, K these 3 sts again; rep from * until tie is 35in/88cm long.
Bind off.
Cuff ties (make 2)
Work as given for neck tie until cuff tie is 31in/78cm long.
Bind off.
See page 124 for finishing instructions, setting in sleeves using the set-in method and leaving side seams open for first 34 rows, and sleeve seams open for first 7 rows.
Fold first 3 rows of body and sleeves, and last 3 rows of neckband, to inside along fold line

rows and slip stitch in place. Thread ties through these casings.

CABLE-YOKE JACKET

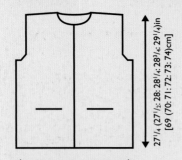

22¹/₂ (23¹/₂: 24¹/₄: 25¹/₂: 26¹/₄: 27¹/₂)in
[57.5 (59.5: 62.5: 64.5: 67.5: 69.5)cm]

27¹/₄ (27¹/₂: 28: 28¹/₄: 28³/₄: 29¹/₄)in
[69 (70: 71: 72: 73: 74)cm]

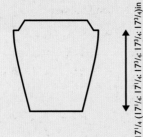

17¹/₄ (17¹/₄: 17¹/₄: 17³/₄: 17³/₄: 17³/₄)in
[44 (44: 44: 45: 45: 45)cm]

SIZES

1	2	3	4	5	6

TO FIT BUST

36	38	40	42	44	46	in
91	97	102	107	112	117	cm

YARN

Rowan Denim—navy (225)

25	26	27	28	29	30 x 50g

NEEDLES

1 pair size 3 (3¼mm) needles
1 pair size 6 (4mm) needles
2 double-pointed size 3 (3¼mm) needles
Cable needle

BUTTONS—7

GAUGE

Before washing: 20 sts and 28 rows to 4in/10cm measured over St st using size 6 (4mm) needles.

Gauge note: Denim will shrink in length when washed for the first time. Allowances have been made in the pattern for shrinkage (see size diagram on the left for after-washing measurements).

SPECIAL ABBREVIATIONS

C6B = slip next 3 sts onto cable needle and leave at back of work, K3, then K3 from cable needle.
C6F = slip next 3 sts onto cable needle and leave at front of work, K3, then K3 from cable needle.

BACK
Tassels

Cast on 3 sts using double-pointed size 3 (3¼mm) needles.
Row 1 (RS): K3, *without turning slip these 3 sts to opposite end of needle and bring yarn to opposite end of work pulling it quite tightly across WS of work, K these 3 sts again, rep

from * until tassel is 4¾in/12cm long. Break yarn and leave sts on a holder. Make a further 36 (38: 40: 42: 44: 46) tassels in this way.

Main section

Using size 3 (3¼mm) needles, cast on 2 (2: 1: 1: 0: 0) sts, (K across 3 tassel sts) 37 (39: 41: 43: 45: 47) times, cast on 2 (2: 1: 1: 0: 0) sts. 115 (121: 125: 131: 135: 141) sts.
Work in garter st for 11 rows, ending with a WS row.
Change to size 6 (4mm) needles.
Row 13 (RS): Knit.
Row 14: K6, P to last 6 sts, K6.
Rep last 2 rows 15 times more.
Beg with a K row, cont in St st until back measures 15 (15¼: 15¼: 16: 16: 16¼)in/38 (39: 39: 40.5: 40.5: 41.5)cm, ending with a WS row.
Work in garter st for 3 rows, ending with a RS row.
Next row (WS) (inc): K14 (17: 19: 22: 24: 27), *(K1, M1) 3 times, K9, rep from * 7 times more, K to end. 139 (145: 149: 155: 159: 165) sts.
Cont in cable patt as foll:
Row 1 (RS): K0 (1: 1: 0: 0: 1), (P1, K1) 7 (8: 9: 11: 12: 13) times, *K6, (K1, P1) 4 times, K1, rep from * 6 times more, K6, (K1, P1) 7 (8: 9: 11: 12: 13) times, K0 (1: 1: 0: 0: 1).
Row 2 and every foll alt row: K0 (1: 1: 0: 0: 1), (P1, K1) 7 (8: 9: 11: 12: 13) times, *P6, (K1, P1) 4 times, K1, rep from * 6 times more, P6, (K1, P1) 7 (8: 9: 11: 12: 13) times, K0 (1: 1: 0: 0: 1).
Row 3: K0 (1: 1: 0: 0: 1), (P1, K1) 7 (8: 9: 11: 12: 13) times, *C6B, (K1, P1) 4 times, K1, rep from * 3 times more, **C6F, (K1, P1) 4 times, K1, rep from ** twice more, C6F, (K1, P1) 7 (8: 9: 11: 12: 13) times, K0 (1: 1: 0: 0: 1).
Rows 5 and 7: Rep row 1.
Row 9: K0 (1: 1: 0: 0: 1), (P1, K1) 7 (8: 9: 11: 12: 13) times, *C6F, (K1, P1) 4 times, K1, rep from * 3 times more, **C6B, (K1, P1) 4 times, K1, rep from ** twice more, C6B, (K1, P1) 7 (8: 9: 11: 12: 13) times, K0 (1: 1: 0: 0: 1).
Row 11: Rep row 1.

Row 12: Rep row 2.

These 12 rows form patt.

Cont in patt until back measures 21 (21½: 21¾: 22: 22: 22¼)in/53.5 (55: 55: 56: 56: 57)cm, ending with a WS row.

Shape armholes

Keeping patt correct, bind off 6 sts at beg of next 2 rows. 127 (133: 137: 143: 147: 153) sts.

Dec 1 st at each end of next and foll 5 alt rows. 115 (121: 125: 131: 135: 141) sts.

Work even until armhole measures 10¾ (10¾: 11: 11: 11½: 11½)in/27 (27: 28: 28: 29: 29)cm, ending with a WS row.

Shape shoulders and back neck

Bind off 13 (14: 15: 15: 16: 17) sts at beg of next 2 rows. 89 (93: 97: 101: 103: 107) sts.

Next row (RS): Bind off 13 (14: 14: 15: 16: 17) sts, patt until there are 17 (17: 19: 20: 19: 20) sts on right needle and turn, leaving rem sts on a holder.

Work each side of neck separately.

Bind off 4 sts at beg of next row.

Bind off rem 13 (13: 15: 16: 15: 16) sts.

With RS facing, rejoin yarn to rem sts, bind off center 29 (31: 31: 31: 33: 33) sts, patt to end.

Complete to match first side, reversing shapings.

POCKET LININGS (make 2)

Cast on 33 sts using size 6 (4mm) needles.

Beg with a K row, work in St st for 50 rows, ending with a WS row.

Break yarn and leave sts on a holder.

LEFT FRONT

Tassels

Make 21 (22: 23: 24: 25: 26) tassels as given for back.

Main section

Using size 3 (3¼mm) needles, cast on 2 (2: 1: 1: 0: 0) sts, (K across 3 tassel sts) 21 (22: 23: 24: 25: 26) times, cast on 1 st. 66 (69: 71: 74: 76: 79) sts.

Work in garter st for 10 rows, ending with a RS row.

Row 12 (WS): K8 and slip these sts onto a holder, K to end. 58 (61: 63: 66: 68: 71) sts.

Change to size 6 (4mm) needles.

Row 13 (RS): Knit.

Row 14: P to last 6 sts, K6.

Rep last 2 rows 15 times more.

Beg with a K row, work in St st for 18 rows, ending with a WS row.

Place pocket

Next row (RS): K12 (14: 15: 16: 17: 19), slip next 33 sts onto a holder and, in their place, K across 33 sts of first pocket lining, K to end.

Cont in St st until left front measures 15 (15¼: 15¼: 16: 16: 16¼)in/38 (39: 39: 40.5: 40.5: 41.5)cm, ending with a WS row.

Work in garter st for 3 rows, ending with a RS row.

Next row (WS) (inc): K5, *(K1, M1) 3 times, K9, rep from * 3 times more, K to end. 70 (73: 75: 78: 80: 83) sts.

Cont in cable patt as foll:

Row 1 (RS): K0 (1: 1: 0: 0: 1), (P1, K1) 7 (8: 9: 11: 12: 13) times, *K6, (K1, P1) 4 times, K1, rep from * twice more, K6, (K1, P1) twice, K1.

Row 2 and every foll alt row: K1, (P1, K1) twice, *P6, (K1, P1) 4 times, K1, rep from * twice more, P6, (K1, P1) 7 (8: 9: 11: 12: 13) times, K0 (1: 1: 0: 0: 1).

Row 3: K0 (1: 1: 0: 0: 1), (P1, K1) 7 (8: 9: 11: 12: 13) times, *C6B, (K1, P1) 4 times, K1, rep from * twice more, C6B, (K1, P1) twice, K1.

Rows 5 and 7: Rep row 1.

Row 9: K0 (1: 1: 0: 0: 1), (P1, K1) 7 (8: 9: 11: 12: 13) times, *C6F, (K1, P1) 4 times, K1, rep from * twice more, C6F, (K1, P1) twice, K1.

Rows 11 and 12: Rep rows 1 and 2.

These 12 rows form patt.

Cont in patt until left front matches back to beg of armhole shaping, ending with a WS row.

Shape armhole

Keeping patt correct, bind off 6 sts at beg of next row. 64 (67: 69: 72: 74: 77) sts.

Work 1 row.

Dec 1 st at armhole edge of next and foll 5 alt rows. 58 (61: 63: 66: 68: 71) sts.

Work even until 15 (17: 17: 17: 17: 17) rows

less have been worked than on back to start of shoulder shaping, ending with a RS row.

Shape neck

Keeping patt correct, bind off 9 (9: 9: 9: 10: 10) sts at beg of next row. 49 (52: 54: 57: 58: 61) sts.

Dec 1 st at neck edge of next 8 rows, then on foll 1 (2: 2: 2: 2: 2) alt rows, then on foll 4th row, ending with a WS row. 39 (41: 43: 46: 47: 50) sts.

Shape shoulder

Bind off 13 (14: 14: 15: 16: 17) sts at beg of next and foll alt row.

Work 1 row.

Bind off rem 13 (13: 15: 16: 15: 16) sts.

RIGHT FRONT

Tassels

Make 21 (22: 23: 24: 25: 26) tassels as given for back.

Main section

Using size 3 (3¼mm) needles, cast on 1 st, (K across 3 tassel sts) 21 (22: 23: 24: 25: 26) times, cast on 2 (2: 1: 1: 0: 0) sts. 66 (69: 71: 74: 76: 79) sts.

Work in garter st for 10 rows, ending with a RS row.

Row 12 (WS): K to last 8 sts and turn, leaving rem 8 sts on a holder. 58 (61: 63: 66: 68: 71) sts.

Change to size 6 (4mm) needles.

Row 13 (RS): Knit.

Row 14: K6, P to end.

Rep last 2 rows 15 times more.

Beg with a K row, work in St st for 18 rows, ending with a WS row.

Place pocket

Next row (RS): K13 (14: 15: 17: 18: 19), slip next 33 sts onto a holder and, in their place, K across 33 sts of second pocket lining, K to end.

Cont in St st until right front measures 15 (15¼: 15¼: 16: 16: 16¼)in/38 (39: 39: 40.5: 40.5: 41.5)cm, ending with a WS row.

Work in garter st for 3 rows, ending with a RS row.

Next row (WS) (inc): K14 (17: 19: 22: 24: 27), *(K1, M1) 3 times, K9, rep from * twice more, (K1, M1) 3 times, K to end. 70 (73: 75: 78: 80: 83) sts.

Cont in cable patt as foll:

Row 1 (RS): K1, (P1, K1) twice, *K6, (K1, P1) 4 times, K1, rep from * twice more, K6, (K1, P1) 7 (8: 9: 11: 12: 13) times, K0 (1: 1: 0: 0: 1).

Row 2 and every foll alt row: K0 (1: 1: 0: 0: 1), (P1, K1) 7 (8: 9: 11: 12: 13) times, *P6, (K1, P1) 4 times, K1, rep from * twice more, P6, (K1, P1) twice, K1.

Row 3: K1, (P1, K1) twice, *C6F, (K1, P1) 4 times, K1, rep from * twice more, C6F, (K1, P1) 7 (8: 9: 11: 12: 13) times, K0 (1: 1: 0: 0: 1).

Rows 5 and 7: Rep row 1.

Row 9: K1, (P1, K1) twice, *C6B, (K1, P1) 4 times, K1, rep from ** twice more, C6B, (K1, P1) 7 (8: 9: 11: 12: 13) times, K0 (1: 1: 0: 0: 1).

Row 11: Rep row 1.

Row 12: Rep row 2.

These 12 rows form patt.

Complete to match left front, reversing shapings.

SLEEVES (both alike)

Cast on 53 (55: 55: 57: 59: 59) sts using size 3 (3¼mm) needles.

Work in garter st for 12 rows, ending with a WS row.

Change to size 6 (4mm) needles.

Beg with a K row, cont in St st, inc 1 st at each end of next and every foll 6th (6th: 4th: 6th: 6th: 6th) row to 83 (83: 59: 87: 89: 89) sts, then on every foll - (-: 6th: -: -: -) row until there are - (-: 85: -: -: -) sts.

Work 1 (7: 3: 1: 1: 1) rows, ending with a WS row.

Work in garter st for 3 rows, inc 0 (1: 1: 0: 0: 0) st at each end of 0 (first: 3rd: 0: 0: 0) of these rows and ending with a RS row. 83 (85: 87: 87: 89: 89) sts.

Next row (WS) (inc): K22 (23: 24: 24: 25: 25), *(K1, M1) 3 times, K9, rep from * twice more, (K1, M1) 3 times, K to end. 95 (97: 99: 99: 101: 101) sts.

Cont in cable patt as foll:

Row 1 (RS): (Inc in first st) 1 (0: 0: 1: 1: 1) times, K1 (1: 0: 1: 0: 0), (P1, K1) 10 (11: 12: 11: 12: 12) times, *K6, (K1, P1) 4 times, K1, rep from * twice more, K6, (K1, P1) 10 (11: 12: 11: 12: 12) times, K1 (1: 0: 1: 0: 0), (inc in last st) 1 (0: 0: 1: 1: 1) times. 97 (97: 99: 101: 103: 103) sts.

Row 2: K1 (1: 0: 1: 0: 0), (P1, K1) 11 (11: 12: 12: 13: 13) times, *P6, (K1, P1) 4 times, K1, rep from * twice more, P6, (K1, P1) 11 (11: 12: 12: 13: 13) times, K1 (1: 0: 1: 0: 0).

Row 3: K1 (1: 0: 1: 0: 0), (P1, K1) 11 (11: 12: 12: 13: 13) times, *C6B, (K1, P1) 4 times, K1, rep from * once more, C6F, (K1, P1) 4 times, K1, C6F, (K1, P1) 11 (11: 12: 12: 13: 13) times, K1 (1: 0: 1: 0: 0).

Row 4: Rep row 2.

Row 5: (Inc in first st) 0 (1: 1: 0: 0: 0) times, K1 (0: 1: 1: 0: 0), (P1, K1) 11 (11: 11: 12: 13: 13) times, *K6, (K1, P1) 4 times, K1, rep from * twice more, K6, (K1, P1) 11 (11: 11: 12: 13: 13) times, K1 (0: 1: 1: 0: 0), (inc in last st) 0 (1: 1: 0: 0: 0) times. 97 (99: 101: 101: 103: 103) sts.

Row 6: K1 (0: 1: 1: 0: 0), (P1, K1) 11 (12: 12: 12: 13: 13) times, *P6, (K1, P1) 4 times, K1, rep from * twice more, P6, (K1, P1) 11 (12: 12: 12: 13: 13) times, K1 (0: 1: 1: 0: 0).

Row 7: (Inc in first st) 1 (0: 0: 1: 1: 1) times, K0 (0: 1: 0: 1: 1), (P1, K1) 11 (12: 12: 12: 12: 12) times, *K6, (K1, P1) 4 times, K1, rep from * twice more, K6, (K1, P1) 11 (12: 12: 12: 12: 12) times, K0 (0: 1: 0: 1: 1), (inc in last st) 1 (0: 0: 1: 1: 1) times. 99 (99: 101: 103: 105: 105) sts.

Row 8: K0 (0: 1: 0: 1: 1), (P1, K1) 12 (12: 12: 13: 13: 13) times, *P6, (K1, P1) 4 times, K1, rep from * twice more, P6, (K1, P1) 12 (12: 12: 13: 13: 13) times, K0 (0: 1: 0: 1: 1).

Row 9: K0 (0: 1: 0: 1: 1), (P1, K1) 12 (12: 12: 13: 13: 13) times, *C6F, (K1, P1) 4 times, K1, rep from * once more, C6B, (K1, P1) 4 times, K1, C6B, (K1, P1) 12 (12: 12: 13: 13: 13) times, K0 (0: 1: 0: 1: 1).

Row 10: Rep row 8.

Row 11: (Inc in first st) 0 (0: 1: 0: 0: 0) times, K0 (0: 0: 0: 1: 1), (P1, K1) 12 (12: 12: 13: 13: 13) times, *K6, (K1, P1) 4 times, K1, rep from * twice more, K6, (K1, P1) 12 (12: 12: 13: 13: 13) times, K0 (0: 0: 0: 1: 1), (inc in last st) 0 (0: 1: 0: 0: 0) times. 99 (99: 103: 103: 105: 105) sts.

Row 12: K0 (0: 0: 0: 1: 1), (P1, K1) 12 (12: 13: 13: 13: 13) times, *P6, (K1, P1) 4 times, K1, rep from * twice more, P6, (K1, P1) 12 (12: 13: 13: 13: 13) times, K0 (0: 0: 0: 1: 1).

These 12 rows form patt and cont sleeve shaping.

Cont in patt, shaping sides by inc 1 st at each end of next (next: 5th: 3rd: next: next) and every foll 8th (8th: 6th: 8th: 6th: 6th) row until there are 105 (105: 109: 109: 113: 113) sts, taking inc sts into seed st.

Work even until sleeve measures 20¼ (20¼: 20¼: 20¾: 20¾: 20¾)in/51.5 (51.5: 51.5: 52.5: 52.5: 52.5)cm, ending with a WS row.

Shape top of sleeve

Keeping patt correct, bind off 6 sts at beg of next 2 rows. 93 (93: 97: 97: 101: 101) sts.

Dec 1 st at each end of next and foll 5 alt rows, then on foll row, ending with a WS row. Bind off rem 79 (79: 83: 83: 87: 87) sts.

FINISHING

Do NOT press.

Join both shoulder seams using backstitch, or mattress stitch if preferred.

Left front band

Slip 8 sts from left front holder onto size 3 (3¼mm) needles and rejoin yarn with RS facing.

Cont in garter st until band, when slightly stretched, fits up left front opening edge to neck shaping, ending with a WS row.

Break yarn and leave sts on a holder.

Slip stitch band in place.

Mark positions for 6 buttons on this band section—first to come 7in/18cm up from lower edge, last to come ½in/1cm below neck shaping, and rem 4 buttons evenly spaced between.

Right front band

Slip 8 sts from right front holder onto size 3 (3¼mm) needles and rejoin yarn with WS facing.

Cont in garter st until band, when slightly stretched, fits up right front opening edge to neck shaping, ending with a WS row and with the addition of 6 buttonholes worked as foll:
Buttonhole row (RS): K3, K2tog, yo (to make a buttonhole), K3.
When band is complete, do NOT break yarn. Slip stitch band in place.

Collar
With RS facing and using size 3 (3¼mm) needles, K 8 from right front band, pick up and knit 24 (26: 26: 26: 27: 27) sts up right side of neck, 31 (33: 33: 33: 34: 34) sts from back, and 24 (26: 26: 26: 27: 27) sts down left side of neck, then K 8 from left front band. 95 (101: 101: 101: 104: 104) sts.
Work in garter st for 3 rows, ending with a WS row.
Next row (RS of body): K3, K2tog, yo (to make 7th buttonhole), K to end.
Work in garter st for a further 4 rows.
Bind off 4 sts at beg of next 2 rows. 87 (93: 93: 93: 96: 96) sts.
Cont in garter st until collar measures 4¾in/12cm from pick-up row, ending with RS of collar (WS of body) facing for next row.
Using size 3 (3¼mm) double-pointed needles, work tassel bind-off as foll: K3, *(without turning slip these 3 sts to opposite end of needle and bring yarn to opposite end of work pulling it quite tightly across WS of work, K these 3 sts again) until tassel is 4¾in/12cm long, without turning slip these 3 sts to opposite end of needle and bring yarn to opposite end of work pulling it quite tightly across WS of work, K3tog and fasten off, K next 3 sts of collar, rep from * until all sts have been bound off.

Pocket tops (both alike)
Slip 33 sts from pocket holder onto size 3 (3¼mm) needles and rejoin yarn with RS facing.
Work in garter st for 12 rows.
Bind off knitwise (on WS).
Machine wash all pieces before completing sewing together.

See page 124 for finishing instructions, setting in sleeves using the shallow set-in method and leaving side seams open for first 44 rows.
Tie a knot in end of each tassel.

NATURAL COLORS

This summery color palette focuses on soft creams and beiges, with the addition of earth tones, to provide very wearable and adaptable designs for all occasions, including textured jackets, smart tops, a range of traditional sweaters, and even a great poncho! The emphasis is on cotton yarns in this section.

Right This little sleeveless Leaf-trim Top, knitted in a lightweight cotton yarn, is ideal for summer. It has an attractive leaf-motif hem and soft cowl neckline. (Instructions on page 72).

Far right This cabled, edge-to-edge, hip-length Herringbone Jacket is knitted in a double-knitting-weight merino wool. It makes the perfect summer cover-up, and is versatile enough to be dressed up for an evening out. (Instructions on page 76.)

Far left *Another great classic cable design, this smart traditional Cable-trim Jacket is knitted in chunky merino wool. Wear it over a classic T-shirt or with the sleeveless tops shown center and near left. (Instructions on page 80.)*

Center left *With a row of little lace heart motifs above the ribbed hem and a knitted scalloped neck edging, the Lace-heart Top would pair well with many of the jackets in the book. It is worked in a super-soft cotton yarn. (Instructions on page 74.)*

Near left *The Plain V-neck Top, also shown on page 60, is worked in a soft, lightweight merino wool. The round-neck version of this plain top is shown with the Mesh Scarf on page 105. (Instructions on page 78.)*

Left *A pretty edging around the neck, armholes, and hem of the V-neck Top gives it a special finishing touch. (Instructions on page 78.)*

Above (left to right) *The Bobble-trim, Tassel-trim, and Cable-trim Sweaters are variations on the classic off-white sweater, in three different cotton yarns.*

All are easy-to-wear hip-length sweaters, with stylish finishing touches. (Instructions on page 82–87.)

Above A clever variation on the classic afghan crochet square creates a smart bag and matching scarf (see opposite). In toning earth shades that harmonize well with most colors, the Motif Bag is a great project for both crochet lovers and those recently converted to the technique. (Instructions on page 88.)

Above *Pair the Motif Scarf, worked in an extra-fine merino wool, with the matching bag or use it on its own to liven up a plain top or jacket. (Instructions on page 89.)*

Above The Garter-rib Sweater is the warm, comfortable cotton knit we all want in our wardrobe, for walks in the country or for lounging by the fire. (Instructions on page 92.)

Right A must-have design and the world's greatest cover up! This classic Tweed Poncho is knitted in stockinette stitch in a chunky wool-mix yarn. It features a cozy rolled collar and a stylish long fringed yoke and hem. (Instructions on page 94.)

Left This smart little seed-stitch Bobble-trim Scarf, with its lacy crocheted bobble edging, is very quick and easy to work. Make it full length or as a short muffler. (Instructions on page 90.)

Above *In an extra-soft, lofty cotton-mix yarn, the Cabled Scarf is a popular classic. It also makes the ideal project for newcomers to cable knitting! (Instructions on page 91.)*

Above The Beaded Jacket above and the textured version on page 20 are both really versatile designs. Worked in an extra-fine merino, they can be worn with a skirt or smart pair of trousers to the office but are also ideal, as here, for country walks. (Instructions on page 96.)

Above: A classic turtleneck design, the Diamond-pattern Sweater is knitted in a lightweight merino wool. The textured pattern is worked from a chart and is formed with simple knit and purl stitches. (Instructions on page 100.)

Above: *This retro-style Zigzag Scarf in four toning colors of soft merino wool is easier to make than it looks. The zigzag pattern stitch, with its very simple two-row repeat, is quickly memorized.*
(Instructions on page 95.)

LEAF-TRIM TOP

24¾ (25: 25½: 26: 26½: 26¾)in
[63 (64: 65: 66: 67: 68)cm]

20 (20¾: 21¾: 22¾: 23¾: 24½)in
[50.5 (52.5: 55.5: 57.5: 60.5: 62.5)cm]

SIZES

1	2	3	4	5	6

TO FIT BUST

36	38	40	42	44	46	in
91	97	102	107	112	117	cm

YARN

Rowan 4 ply Cotton—ecru (112)

7	8	8	9	9	10 x 50g

NEEDLES

1 pair size 1 (2¼mm) needles
1 pair size 2 (2¾mm) needles
1 pair size 3 (3mm) needles

GAUGE

28 sts and 38 rows to 4in/10cm measured over St st using size 3 (3mm) needles.

BACK

Cast on 141 (147: 155: 161: 169: 175) sts using size 1 (2¼mm) needles.
Row 1 (RS): P0 (3: 0: 3: 0: 3), K1, *yo, P5, P3tog, P5, yo, K1, rep from * to last 0 (3: 0: 3: 0: 3) sts, P0 (3: 0: 3: 0: 3).
Row 2 and every foll alt row: Purl.
Rows 3, 5, 7, 9, and 11: Rep row 1.
Change to size 2 (2¾mm) needles.
Row 13: K1 (4: 1: 4: 1: 4), *yo, skp, yo, P3, P3tog, P3, yo, K2tog, yo, K1, rep from * to last 0 (3: 0: 3: 0: 3) sts, K0 (3: 0: 3: 0: 3).
Row 15: K1 (4: 1: 4: 1: 4), *yo, K1, skp, yo, P2, P3tog, P2, yo, K2tog, K1, yo, K1, rep from * to last 0 (3: 0: 3: 0: 3) sts, K0 (3: 0: 3: 0: 3).
Row 17: K1 (4: 1: 4: 1: 4), *yo, K2, skp, yo, P1, P3tog, P1, yo, K2tog, K2, yo, K1, rep from * to last 0 (3: 0: 3: 0: 3) sts, K0 (3: 0: 3: 0: 3).
Row 19: K1 (4: 1: 4: 1: 4), *yo, K3, skp, yo, P3tog, yo, K2tog, K3, yo, K1, rep from * to last 0 (3: 0: 3: 0: 3) sts, K0 (3: 0: 3: 0: 3).
Change to size 3 (3mm) needles.
Row 21: K1 (4: 1: 4: 1: 4), *K3, K2tog, yo, K3, yo, skp, K4, rep from * to last 0 (3: 0: 3: 0: 3) sts, K0 (3: 0: 3: 0: 3).
Row 23: K1 (4: 1: 4: 1: 4), *K2, K2tog, yo, K5,

yo, skp, K3, rep from * to last 0 (3: 0: 3: 0: 3) sts, K0 (3: 0: 3: 0: 3).
Row 25: K1 (4: 1: 4: 1: 4), *K1, K2tog, yo, K7, yo, skp, K2, rep from * to last 0 (3: 0: 3: 0: 3) sts, K0 (3: 0: 3: 0: 3).
Row 27: K1 (4: 1: 4: 1: 4), *K2tog, yo, K9, yo, skp, K1, rep from * to last 0 (3: 0: 3: 0: 3) sts, K0 (3: 0: 3: 0: 3).
Row 29: K0 (3: 0: 3: 0: 3), K2tog, yo, *K11, yo, sl 1, K2tog, psso, yo, rep from * to last 13 (16: 13: 16: 13: 16) sts, K11, yo, skp, K0 (3: 0: 3: 0: 3).
Row 30: Rep row 2.
These 30 rows complete border patt.
Beg with a K row, cont in St st until back measures 4 (4¼: 4¼: 4¾: 5: 5¼)in/10 (11: 11: 12: 12: 13)cm, ending with a WS row.
Dec 1 st at each end of next and every foll 10th row until 129 (135: 143: 149: 157: 163) sts rem.
Work 9 rows, ending with a WS row.
Inc 1 st at each end of next and every foll 10th row until there are 141 (147: 155: 161: 169: 175) sts.
Work even until back measures 16½ (16¾: 16¾: 17¼: 17½: 17¾)in/42 (43: 43: 44: 44: 45)cm, ending with a WS row.
Shape armholes
Bind off 7 (8: 8: 9: 9: 10) sts at beg of next 2 rows. 127 (131: 139: 143: 151: 155) sts.
Dec 1 st at each end of next 9 (9: 11: 11: 13: 13) rows, then on foll 7 (8: 8: 9: 9: 10) alt rows, then on foll 4th row. 93 (95: 99: 101: 105: 107) sts.
Work even until armhole measures 8¼ (8¼: 8¾: 8¾: 9: 9)in/21 (21: 22: 22: 23: 23)cm, ending with a WS row.
Shape shoulders and back neck
Bind off 5 (5: 6: 6: 6: 7) sts at beg of next 2 rows. 83 (85: 87: 89: 93: 93) sts.
Next row (RS): Bind off 5 (5: 6: 6: 6: 7) sts, K until there are 9 (9: 9: 10: 11: 10) sts on right needle and turn, leaving rem sts on a holder.
Work each side of neck separately.
Bind off 4 sts at beg of next row.
Bind off rem 5 (5: 5: 6: 7: 6) sts.

With RS facing, rejoin yarn to rem sts, bind off center 55 (57: 57: 57: 59: 59) sts, K to end. Complete to match first side, reversing shapings.

FRONT

Work as given for back until 14 (16: 16: 16: 16: 16) rows less have been worked than on back to start of shoulder shaping, ending with a WS row.

Shape neck

Next row (RS): K27 (28: 30: 31: 32: 33) and turn, leaving rem sts on a holder.

Work each side of neck separately.

Bind off 5 sts at beg of next row. 22 (23: 25: 26: 27: 28) sts.

Dec 1 st at neck edge of next 3 rows, then on foll 4 (5: 5: 5: 5: 5) alt rows. 15 (15: 17: 18: 19: 20) sts.

Work 1 row, ending with a WS row.

Shape shoulder

Bind off 5 (5: 6: 6: 6: 7) sts at beg of next and foll alt row.

Work 1 row.

Bind off rem 5 (5: 5: 6: 7: 6) sts.

With RS facing, rejoin yarn to rem sts, bind off center 39 (39: 39: 39: 41: 41) sts, K to end.

Complete to match first side, reversing shapings.

FINISHING

BLOCK as described on page 123.

Join both shoulder seams using backstitch, or mattress stitch if preferred.

Armhole borders (both alike)

With RS facing and using size 1 (2¼mm) needles, pick up and knit 130 (132: 138: 140: 146: 148) sts all round armhole edge.

Work in garter st for 2 rows.

Bind off knitwise (on WS).

Collar

Cast on 169 (169: 183: 183: 197: 197) sts using size 1 (2¼mm) needles.

Row 1 (RS): K1, *yo, P5, P3tog, P5, yo, K1, rep from * to end.

Row 2 and every foll alt row: Purl.

Rows 3, 5, 7, 9, and 11: Rep row 1.

Change to size 2 (2¾mm) needles.

Row 13: K1, *yo, skp, yo, P3, P3tog, P3, yo, K2tog, yo, K1, rep from * to end.

Row 15: K1, *yo, K1, skp, yo, P2, P3tog, P2, yo, K2tog, K1, yo, K1, rep from * to end.

Row 17: K1, *yo, K2, skp, yo, P1, P3tog, P1, yo, K2tog, K2, yo, K1, rep from * to end.

Row 19: K1, *yo, K3, skp, yo, P3tog, yo, K2tog, K3, yo, K1, rep from * to end.

Change to size 3 (3mm) needles.

Row 21: K1, *K3, K2tog, yo, K3, yo, skp, K4, rep from * to end.

Row 23: K1, *K2, K2tog, yo, K5, yo, skp, K3, rep from * to end.

Row 25: K1, *K1, K2tog, yo, K7, yo, skp, K2, rep from * to end.

Row 27: K1, *K2tog, yo, K9, yo, skp, K1, rep from * to end.

Row 29: K2tog, yo, *K11, yo, sl 1, K2tog, psso, yo, rep from * to last 13 sts, K11, yo, skp.

Row 30: Rep row 2.

These 30 rows complete border patt.

Beg with a K row, cont in St st for 16 rows, ending with a WS row.

Change to size 2 (2¾mm) needles.

Row 47 (RS): K8 (8: 9: 9: 10: 10), K2tog, *K4, K2tog, rep from * to last 9 (9: 10: 10: 11: 11) sts, K to end. 143 (143: 155: 155: 167: 167) sts.

Cont in St st until collar measures 6¾in/17cm, ending with a WS row.

Change to size 1 (2¼mm) needles.

Next row (RS): K8 (8: 9: 9: 10: 10), K2tog, *K3, K2tog, rep from * to last 8 (8: 9: 9: 10: 10) sts, K to end. 117 (117: 127: 127: 137: 137) sts.

Cont in St st until collar measures 9½in/24cm, ending with a WS row.

Bind off knitwise.

Join row-end edges of collar. Placing seam at center back neck and easing in slight fullness, sew bound-off edge of collar to neck edge.

See page 124 for finishing instructions.

LACE-HEART TOP

24¾ (25: 25½: 26: 26½: 26¾)in
[63 (64: 65: 66: 67: 68)cm]

19½ (20½: 21½: 22½: 24: 25)in
[49 (52: 55: 57.5: 60.5: 63.5)cm]

SIZES

1	2	3	4	5	6

TO FIT BUST

| 36 | 38 | 40 | 42 | 44 | 46 | in |
| 91 | 97 | 102 | 107 | 112 | 117 | cm |

YARN

Rowan Calmer—coffee bean (481)

6	6	7	7	8	8 x 50g

NEEDLES

1 pair size 6 (4mm) needles
1 pair size 8 (5mm) needles

GAUGE

21 sts and 30 rows to 4in/10cm measured over St st using size 8 (5mm) needles.

SPECIAL ABBREVIATION

dec2 = K2tog and slip st now on right needle back onto left needle, lift 2nd st on left needle over this st and off left needle, then slip same st back onto right needle.

BACK

Cast on 103 (109: 115: 121: 127: 133) sts using size 6 (4mm) needles.
Row 1 (RS): P2, *K3, P3, rep from * to last 5 sts, K3, P2.
Row 2: K2, *P3, K3, rep from * to last 5 sts, P3, K2.
These 2 rows form rib.
Work in rib for a further 4 rows, ending with a WS row.
Change to size 8 (5mm) needles.
Beg with a K row, work in St st for 4 rows, ending with a WS row.
Place heart motifs
Row 5 (RS): K5 (8: 3: 6: 1: 4), work next 13 sts as row 1 of heart motif chart, *K3, work next 13 sts as row 1 of heart motif chart, rep from * to last 5 (8: 3: 6: 1: 4) sts, K to end.
Row 6: P5 (8: 3: 6: 1: 4), work next 13 sts as row 2 of heart motif chart, *P3, work next 13

sts as row 2 of heart motif chart, rep from * to last 5 (8: 3: 6: 1: 4) sts, P to end.
These 2 rows set position of heart motifs on St st.
Cont as set until all 16 rows of heart motif chart have been completed, ending with a WS row.
Beg with a K row, cont in St st, dec 1 st at each end of 15th and every foll 12th row until 95 (101: 107: 113: 119: 125) sts rem.
Work 11 rows, ending with a WS row.
Inc 1 st at each end of next and every foll 10th row until there are 103 (109: 115: 121: 127: 133) sts.
Work even until back measures 16½ (16¾: 16¾: 17¼: 17½: 17¾)in/42 (43: 43: 44: 44: 45)cm, ending with a WS row.
Shape armholes
Bind off 6 (7: 7: 8: 8: 9) sts at beg of next 2 rows. 91 (95: 101: 105: 111: 115) sts.
Dec 1 st at each end of next 5 (5: 7: 7: 9: 9) rows, then on foll 4 (5: 5: 6: 6: 7) alt rows, then on every foll 4th row until 69 (71: 73: 75: 77: 79) sts rem.
Work even until armhole measures 8¼ (8¼: 8¾: 8¾: 9: 9)in/21 (22: 22: 23: 23)cm, ending with a WS row.
Shape shoulders and back neck
Bind off 4 (4: 4: 5: 5: 5) sts at beg of next 2 rows. 61 (63: 65: 65: 67: 69) sts.
Next row (RS): Bind off 4 (4: 4: 5: 5: 5) sts, K until there are 8 (8: 9: 8: 8: 9) sts on right needle and turn, leaving rem sts on a holder.
Work each side of neck separately.
Bind off 4 sts at beg of next row.
Bind off rem 4 (4: 5: 4: 4: 5) sts.
With RS facing, rejoin yarn to rem sts, bind off center 37 (39: 39: 39: 41: 41) sts, K to end.
Complete to match first side, reversing shapings.

FRONT

Work as given for back until 12 (14: 14: 14: 14: 14) rows less have been worked than on back to start of shoulder shaping, ending with a WS row.

Shape neck

Next row (RS): K24 (25: 26: 27: 27: 28) and turn, leaving rem sts on a holder.
Work each side of neck separately.
Bind off 5 sts at beg of next row. 19 (20: 21: 22: 22: 23) sts.
Dec 1 st at neck edge of next 5 rows, then on foll 2 (3: 3: 3: 3: 3) alt rows. 12 (12: 13: 14: 14: 15) sts.
Work 1 row, ending with a WS row.

Shape shoulder

Bind off 4 (4: 4: 5: 5: 5) sts at beg of next and foll alt row.
Work 1 row.
Bind off rem 4 (4: 5: 4: 4: 5) sts.
With RS facing, rejoin yarn to rem sts, bind off center 21 (21: 21: 21: 23: 23) sts, K to end.
Complete to match first side, reversing shapings.

FINISHING

BLOCK as described on page 123.
Join both shoulder seams using backstitch.

Neck trim
Cast on 189 (200: 200: 200: 211: 211) sts using size 6 (4mm) needles.
Row 1 (WS): Purl.
Row 2: K2, *K1 and slip this st back onto left needle, lift the next 8 sts on left needle over this st and off left needle, (yo) twice, K st on left needle again, K2, rep from * to end.
Row 3: K1, *P2tog, (K1, K1 tbl) twice into double yo of previous row, P1, rep from * to last st, K1. 104 (110: 110: 110: 116: 116) sts.
Row 4: Knit.
Bind off knitwise.
Join row-end edges of neck trim, then sew bound-off edge of neck trim to neck edge, positioning seam at center back neck.

Armhole borders (both alike)
With RS facing and using size 6 (4mm) needles, pick up and knit 100 (102: 106: 108: 112: 114) sts all round armhole edge.
Work in garter st for 2 rows.
Bind off knitwise (on WS).
See page 124 for finishing instructions.

Heart motif chart

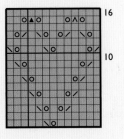

Key

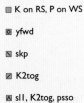

K on RS, P on WS

yfwd

skp

K2tog

sl1, K2tog, psso

dec 2

HERRINGBONE JACKET

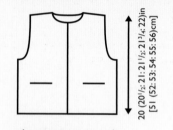

20 (20½: 21: 21½: 21¾: 22)in
[51 (52: 53: 54: 55: 56)cm]

20½ (21½: 22½: 23½: 24½: 25½)in
[52 (54.5: 57: 59.5: 62: 64.5)cm]

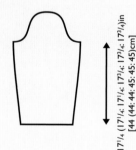

17¼ (17¼: 17¼: 17¾: 17¾: 17¾)in
[44 (44: 44: 45: 45: 45)cm]

SIZES

| 1 | 2 | 3 | 4 | 5 | 6 |

TO FIT BUST

| 36 | 38 | 40 | 42 | 44 | 46 | in |
| 91 | 97 | 102 | 107 | 112 | 117 | cm |

YARN

Jaeger Extra Fine Merino DK—
oatmeal (936)

| 14 | 14 | 15 | 15 | 16 | 16 x 50g |

NEEDLES

1 pair size 3 (3mm) needles
1 pair size 5 (3¾mm) needles
Cable needle

GAUGE

24 sts and 36 rows to 4in/10cm measured over pattern using size 5 (3¾mm) needles.

SPECIAL ABBREVIATIONS

C6B = slip next 3 sts onto cable needle and leave at back of work, K3, then K3 from cable needle.

BACK

Cast on 125 (131: 137: 143: 149: 155) sts using size 5 (3¾mm) needles.
Starting and ending rows as indicated and repeating the 4 row patt rep throughout, cont in patt from chart as foll:
Work even until back measures 10¼ (10¾: 10¾: 11¼: 11¼: 11½)in/26 (27: 27: 28: 28: 29)cm, ending with a WS row.

Shape armholes

Keeping patt correct, bind off 7 (8: 8: 9: 9: 10) sts at beg of next 2 rows. 111 (115: 121: 125: 131: 135) sts.
Dec 1 st at each end of next 3 (3: 5: 5: 7: 7) rows, then on foll 3 (4: 4: 5: 5: 6) alt rows, then on every foll 4th row until 95 (97: 99: 101: 103: 105) sts rem.
Work even until armhole measures 9 (9: 9½: 9½: 9¾: 9¾)in/23 (23: 24: 24: 25: 25)cm, ending with a WS row.

Shape shoulders and back neck

Bind off 9 (9: 10: 10: 10: 10) sts at beg of next 2 rows. 77 (79: 79: 81: 83: 85) sts.
Next row (RS): Bind off 9 (9: 10: 10: 10: 10) sts, patt until there are 14 (14: 13: 14: 14: 15) sts on right needle and turn, leaving rem sts on a holder.
Work each side of neck separately.
Bind off 4 sts at beg of next row.
Bind off rem 10 (10: 9: 10: 10: 11) sts.
With RS facing, rejoin yarn to rem sts, bind off center 31 (33: 33: 33: 35: 35) sts, patt to end.
Complete to match first side, reversing shapings.

POCKET LININGS (make 2)

Cast on 29 sts using size 5 (3¾mm) needles.
Beg with a K row, work in St st for 40 rows, ending with a WS row.
Row 41 (RS): (K10, M1) twice, K9. 31 sts.
Break yarn and leave sts on a holder.

LEFT FRONT

Cast on 60 (63: 66: 69: 72: 75) sts using size 5 (3¾mm) needles.
Starting and ending rows as indicated, cont in patt from chart as foll:
Work 1 row.
Inc 1 st at beg of next row and at same edge on foll 2 rows. 63 (66: 69: 72: 75: 78) sts.
Work even for a further 42 rows, ending with a WS row.

Place pocket

Row 47 (RS): Patt 19 sts, bind off next 31 sts, patt to end.
Row 48: Patt 13 (16: 19: 22: 25: 28) sts, patt across 31 sts of first pocket lining, patt to end.
Work even until left front matches back to beg of armhole shaping, ending with a WS row.

Shape armhole

Keeping patt correct, bind off 7 (8: 8: 9: 9: 10) sts at beg of next row. 56 (58: 61: 63: 66: 68) sts.
Work 1 row.
Dec 1 st at armhole edge of next 3 (3: 5: 5: 7: 7) rows, then on foll 3 (4: 4: 5: 5: 6) alt rows,

then on every foll 4th row until 48 (49: 50: 51: 52: 53) sts rem.
Work even until 19 (21: 21: 21: 21: 21) rows less have been worked than on back to start of shoulder shaping, ending with a RS row.

Shape neck
Keeping patt correct, bind off 9 (9: 9: 9: 10: 10) sts at beg of next row. 39 (40: 41: 42: 42: 43) sts.
Dec 1 st at neck edge of next 6 rows, then on foll 4 (5: 5: 5: 5: 5) alt rows, then on foll 4th row, ending with a WS row. 28 (28: 29: 30: 30: 31) sts.

Shape shoulder
Bind off 9 (9: 10: 10: 10: 10) sts at beg of next and foll alt row.
Work 1 row.
Bind off rem 10 (10: 9: 10: 10: 11) sts.

RIGHT FRONT
Cast on 60 (63: 66: 69: 72: 75) sts using size 5 (3¾mm) needles.
Starting and ending rows as indicated, cont in patt from chart as foll:
Work 1 row.
Inc 1 st at end of next row and at same edge on foll 2 rows. 63 (66: 69: 72: 75: 78) sts.
Work even for a further 42 rows, ending with a WS row.

Place pocket
Row 47 (RS): Patt 13 (16: 19: 22: 25: 28) sts, bind off next 31 sts, patt to end.
Row 48: Patt 19 sts, patt across 31 sts of second pocket lining, patt to end.
Complete to match left front, reversing shapings.

SLEEVES (both alike)
Cast on 63 (65: 65: 67: 69: 69) sts using size 5 (3¾mm) needles.
Starting and ending rows as indicated, cont in patt from chart, inc 1 st at each end of 9th (9th: 7th: 7th: 7th: 7th) and every foll 10th (10th: 8th: 8th: 8th: 8th) row to 85 (87: 71: 71: 73: 83) sts, then on every foll 12th (12th: 10th: 10th: 10th: 10th) row until there are 89 (91: 93: 95: 97: 99) sts, taking inc sts into patt.
Work even until sleeve measures 16½ (16½: 16½: 17: 17: 17)in/42 (42: 42: 43: 43: 43)cm, ending with a WS row.

Shape sleeve cap
Keeping patt correct, bind off 7 (8: 8: 9: 9: 10) sts at beg of next 2 rows. 75 (75: 77: 77: 79: 79) sts.
Dec 1 st at each end of next 5 rows, then on foll 4 alt rows, then on every foll 4th row until 43 (43: 45: 45: 47: 47) sts rem.
Work 1 row, ending with a WS row.
Dec 1 st at each end of next and every foll alt row to 35 sts, then on foll 5 rows, ending with a WS row.
Bind off rem 25 sts.

FINISHING
BLOCK as described on page 123.
Join both shoulder seams using backstitch, or mattress stitch if preferred. Join side seams.

Front edging
Cast on 8 sts using size 3 (3mm) needles.
Row 1 (RS): P2, K6.
Row 2: P6, K2.
Row 3: P2, C6B.

Row 4: Rep row 2.
Rows 5 and 6: Rep rows 1 and 2.
These 6 rows form patt.
Cont in patt until edging fits around entire hem, front opening and neck edges, starting and ending at base of left side seam, easing in fullness around corners to ensure edging lays flat and ending with a WS row.
Bind off.
Slip stitch un-cabled edge in place, joining cast-on and bound-off edges.

Cuff edging (both alike)
Work as given for front edging, working a strip long enough to fit along sleeve cast-on edge.

Pocket edgings (both alike)
Work as given for front edging, working a strip long enough to fit across bound-off edge of pocket opening.

See page 124 for finishing instructions, setting in sleeves using the set-in method.

Key □ K on RS, P on WS   ▣ P on RS, K on WS

4 row patt rep

1st size back & fronts
2nd size back & fronts
3rd size back & fronts
4th size back & fronts
5th size back & fronts
6th size back & fronts

right front   left front
1st size sleeves
2nd, 3rd sizes sleeves
4th size sleeves
5th, 6th sizes sleeves

1st size back & fronts
2nd size back & fronts
3rd size back & fronts
4th size back & fronts
5th size back & fronts
6th size back & fronts

ROUND-NECK AND V-NECK TOPS

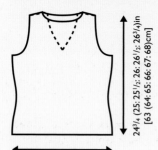

20 (21: 22: 23: 24: 25)in
[50.5 (53: 55.5: 58: 60.5: 63)cm]

24¾ (25: 25½: 26: 26½: 26¾)in
[63 (64: 65: 66: 67: 68)cm]

SIZES

1	2	3	4	5	6

TO FIT BUST

36	38	40	42	44	46	in
91	97	102	107	112	117	cm

YARNS

Rowan 4 ply Soft
ROUND-NECK TOP—light dusty
plum (378)—see page 105

7	7	8	8	8	9 x 50g

V-NECK TOP—expresso (389)—see left

7	7	8	8	8	9 x 50g

NEEDLES AND CROCHET HOOK

1 pair size 2 (2¾mm) needles
1 pair size 3 (3¼mm) needles
V-neck top only: size C-2 (2.50mm) crochet
hook

GAUGE

28 sts and 36 rows to 4in/10cm measured
over St st using size 3 (3¼mm) needles.

CROCHET ABBREVIATIONS

sc = single crochet; **ch** = chain; **dc** = double
crochet.

ROUND-NECK TOP

BACK

Cast on 142 (150: 154: 162: 170: 178) sts using
size 2 (2¾mm) needles.
Row 1 (RS): K2, *P2, K2, rep from * to end.
Row 2: P2, *K2, P2, rep from * to end.
These 2 rows form rib.
Work in rib for a further 4 rows, dec (dec: inc:
inc: dec: dec) 1 st at center of last row and
ending with a WS row. 141 (149: 155: 163: 169:
177) sts.
Change to size 3 (3¼mm) needles.
Beg with a K row, work in St st as foll:
Work 36 rows, ending with a WS row.
Dec 1 st at each end of next and every foll
10th row to 133 (141: 147: 155: 161: 169) sts,

then on every foll 8th row until 129 (137: 143:
151: 157: 165) sts rem.
Work 11 rows, ending with a WS row.
Inc 1 st at each end of next and every foll 8th
row until there are 141 (149: 155: 163: 169:
177) sts.
Work even until back measures 16½ (16¾:
16¾: 17¼: 17½: 17¾)in/42 (43: 43: 44: 44:
45)cm, ending with a WS row.
Shape armholes
Bind off 7 (8: 8: 9: 9: 10) sts at beg of next 2
rows. 127 (133: 139: 145: 151: 157) sts.
Dec 1 st at each end of next 9 (9: 11: 11: 13:
13) rows, then on foll 7 (8: 8: 9: 9: 10) alt rows,
then on foll 4th row. 93 (97: 99: 103: 105:
109) sts.
Work even until armhole measures 8¼ (8¼:
8¾: 8¾: 9: 9)in/21 (21: 22: 22: 23: 23)cm, ending
with a WS row.
Shape shoulders and back neck
Bind off 6 (7: 7: 8: 8: 8) sts at beg of next 2
rows. 81 (83: 85: 87: 89: 93) sts.
Next row (RS): Bind off 6 (7: 7: 8: 8: 8) sts,
K until there are 11 (10: 11: 11: 11: 13) sts
on right needle and turn, leaving rem sts on
a holder.
Work each side of neck separately.
Bind off 4 sts at beg of next row.
Bind off rem 7 (6: 7: 7: 7: 9) sts.
With RS facing, rejoin yarn to rem sts, bind off
center 47 (49: 49: 49: 51: 51) sts, K to end.
Complete to match first side, reversing
shapings.

FRONT

Work as given for back until 24 (26: 26: 26: 26:
26) rows less have been worked than on back
to start of shoulder shaping, ending with a
WS row.
Shape neck
Next row (RS): K 32 (34: 35: 37: 37: 39) sts
and turn, leaving rem sts on a holder.
Work each side of neck separately.
Dec 1 st at neck edge of next 9 rows, then on
foll 1 (2: 2: 2: 2: 2) alt rows, then on every foll
4th row until 19 (20: 21: 23: 23: 25) sts rem,

ending with a WS row.
Shape shoulder
Bind off 6 (7: 7: 8: 8: 8) sts at beg of next and foll alt row.
Work 1 row.
Bind off rem 7 (6: 7: 7: 7: 9) sts.
With RS facing, rejoin yarn to rem sts, bind off center 29 (29: 29: 29: 31: 31) sts, K to end.
Complete to match first side, reversing shapings.

FINISHING
BLOCK as described on page 123.
Join right shoulder seam using backstitch, or mattress stitch if preferred.
Neckband
With RS facing and using size 2 (2¾mm) needles, pick up and knit 23 (24: 24: 24: 24: 24) sts down left side of neck, 29 (29: 29: 29: 31: 31) sts from front, 23 (24: 24: 24: 24: 24) sts up right side of neck, then 55 (57: 57: 57: 59: 59) sts from back. 130 (134: 134: 134: 138: 138) sts.
Beg with row 1, work in rib as given for back for 2 rows.
Bind off in rib (on WS).
Join left shoulder and neckband seam.
Armhole borders (both alike)
With RS facing and using size 2 (2¾mm) needles, pick up and knit 130 (134: 138: 142: 146: 150) sts all round armhole edge.
Beg with row 1, work in rib as given for back for 2 rows.
Bind off in rib (on WS).
See page 124 for finishing instructions.

V-NECK TOP

BACK
Cast on 141 (149: 155: 163: 169: 177) sts using size 3 (3¼mm) needles.
Beg with a K row, work in St st as foll:
Work 36 rows, ending with a WS row.
Dec 1 st at each end of next and every foll 10th row to 133 (141: 147: 155: 161: 169) sts,

then on every foll 8th row until 129 (137: 143: 151: 157: 165) sts rem.
Work 11 rows, ending with a WS row.
Inc 1 st at each end of next and every foll 8th row until there are 141 (149: 155: 163: 169: 177) sts.
Work even until back measures 16 (16¼: 16¼: 16¾: 17: 17¼)in/41 (42: 42: 43: 43: 44)cm, ending with a WS row.
Shape armholes
Bind off 7 (8: 8: 9: 9: 10) sts at beg of next 2 rows. 127 (133: 139: 145: 151: 157) sts.**
Dec 1 st at each end of next 9 (9: 11: 11: 13: 13) rows, then on foll 7 (8: 8: 9: 9: 10) alt rows, then on foll 4th row. 93 (97: 99: 103: 105: 109) sts.
Work even until armhole measures 8¼ (8¼: 8¾: 8¾: 9: 9)in/21 (21: 22: 22: 23: 23)cm, ending with a WS row.
Shape shoulders and back neck
Bind off 8 (8: 9: 9: 9: 10) sts at beg of next 2 rows. 77 (81: 81: 85: 87: 89) sts.
Next row (RS): Bind off 8 (8: 9: 9: 9: 10) sts, K until there are 12 (13: 12: 14: 14: 14) sts on right needle and turn, leaving rem sts on a holder.
Work each side of neck separately.
Bind off 4 sts at beg of next row.
Bind off rem 8 (9: 8: 10: 10: 10) sts.
With RS facing, rejoin yarn to rem sts, bind off center 37 (39: 39: 39: 41: 41) sts, K to end.
Complete to match first side, reversing shapings.

FRONT
Work as given for back to **.
Dec 1 st at each end of next 8 rows, ending with a WS row. 111 (117: 123: 129: 135: 141) sts.
Divide for neck
Next row (RS): K2tog, K53 (56: 59: 62: 65: 68) and turn, leaving rem sts on a holder.
Work each side of neck separately.
Dec 0 (0: 1: 1: 1: 1) st at armhole edge of next row. 54 (57: 59: 62: 65: 68) sts.
Dec 1 st at armhole edge of next 1 (1: 1: 1: 3: 3) rows, then on foll 6 (7: 8: 9: 9: 10) alt rows,

then on foll 4th row **and at same time** dec 1 st at neck edge on next and every foll alt row. 37 (38: 38: 39: 39: 40) sts.
Dec 1 st at neck edge **only** on 2nd and foll 6 (7: 4: 3: 3: 2) alt rows, then on every foll 4th row until 24 (25: 26: 28: 28: 30) sts rem.
Work even until front matches back to start of shoulder shaping, ending with a WS row.
Shape shoulder
Bind off 8 (8: 9: 9: 9: 10) sts at beg of next and foll alt row.
Work 1 row.
Bind off rem 8 (9: 8: 10: 10: 10) sts.
With RS facing, rejoin yarn to rem sts, K2tog, K to last 2 sts, K2tog.
Complete to match first side, reversing shapings.

FINISHING
BLOCK as described on page 123.
Join shoulder seams using backstitch, or mattress stitch if preferred.
See page 124 for finishing instructions.
Edging
With size C-2 (2.50mm) crochet hook and RS facing, attach yarn to neck edge at one shoulder seam, ch1 (does NOT count as st), work one round of sc evenly around entire neck edge, working an even number of sts and ending with 1 slip st in first sc.
Next round (RS): Ch4 (counts as 1dc and ch1), (1dc, ch1) 3 times into front loop only of sc at base of 4ch, (ch1, 1dc) 3 times into back loop only of same sc, 1dc into back loop of same sc, *skip 1sc, (1dc, ch1) 4 times into front loop only of next sc, (1dc, ch1) 3 times into back loop only of same st, 1dc into back loop of same sc, rep from * to last sc, skip last sc, 1 slip st in 3rd of 4ch at beg of round.
Fasten off.
Work edging around armhole and lower edges in same way.

CABLE-TRIM JACKET

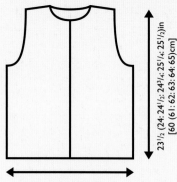

20¾ (22: 23: 24: 25: 26)in
[52.5 (55.5: 58: 60.5: 63.5: 66)cm]

23½ (24: 24½: 24¼: 25¼: 25½)in
[60 (61: 62: 63: 64: 65)cm]

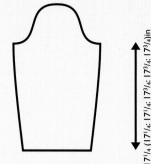

17¼ (17¼: 17¼: 17¾: 17¾: 17¾)in
[44 (44: 44: 45: 45: 45)cm]

SIZES

| 1 | 2 | 3 | 4 | 5 | 6 |

TO FIT BUST

| 36 | 38 | 40 | 42 | 44 | 46 | in |
| 91 | 97 | 102 | 107 | 112 | 117 | cm |

YARN

Jaeger Extra Fine Merino Chunky—
chocolate brown (022)

| 17 | 17 | 18 | 19 | 20 | 20 x 50g |

NEEDLES

1 pair size 8 (5mm) needles
1 pair size 10 (6mm) needles
Cable needle

EXTRAS—1 decorative pin or brooch

GAUGE

15 sts and 20 rows to 4in/10cm measured over St st using size 10 (6mm) needles.

SPECIAL ABBREVIATION

C4B = slip next 2 sts onto cable needle and leave at back of work, K2, then K2 from cable needle.

BACK

Cast on 79 (83: 87: 91: 95: 99) sts using size 8 (5mm) needles.
Work in garter st for 6 rows, ending with a WS row.
Change to size 10 (6mm) needles.
Row 7 (RS): Knit.
Row 8: K4, P to last 4 sts, K4.
Rep last 2 rows 7 times more.
Beg with a K row, cont in St st until back measures 14½ (15: 15: 15¼: 15½: 15¾)in/ 37 (38: 38: 39: 39: 40)cm, ending with a WS row.
Shape armholes
Bind off 4 (5: 5: 6: 6: 7) sts at beg of next 2 rows. 71 (73: 77: 79: 83: 85) sts.
Next row (RS): K2, K2tog, K to last 4 sts, K2tog tbl, K2.

Next row: P2, P2tog tbl, P to last 4 sts, P2tog, P2.
Working all decreases as set by last 2 rows, dec 1 st at each end of next 1 (1: 3: 3: 5: 5) rows, then on foll 3 alt rows, then on every foll 4th row until 55 (57: 57: 59: 59: 61) sts rem.
Work even until armhole measures 9 (9: 9½: 9½: 9¾: 9¾)in/23 (23: 24: 24: 25: 25)cm, ending with a WS row.
Shape shoulders and back neck
Bind off 5 (5: 5: 6: 5: 6) sts at beg of next 2 rows. 45 (47: 47: 47: 49: 49) sts.
Next row (RS): Bind off 5 (5: 5: 6: 5: 6) sts, K until there are 10 (10: 10: 9: 10: 9) sts on right needle and turn, leaving rem sts on a holder.
Work each side of neck separately.
Bind off 4 sts at beg of next row.
Bind off rem 6 (6: 6: 5: 6: 5) sts.
With RS facing, rejoin yarn to rem sts, bind off center 15 (17: 17: 17: 19: 19) sts, K to end.
Complete to match first side, reversing shapings.

LEFT FRONT

Cast on 40 (42: 44: 46: 48: 50) sts using size 8 (5mm) needles.
Work in garter st for 6 rows, ending with a WS row.
Change to size 10 (6mm) needles.
Row 7 (RS): Knit.
Row 8: P to last 4 sts, K4.
Rep last 2 rows 7 times more.
Beg with a K row, cont in St st until left front matches back to beg of armhole shaping, ending with a WS row.
Shape armhole
Bind off 4 (5: 5: 6: 6: 7) sts at beg of next row. 36 (37: 39: 40: 42: 43) sts.
Work 1 row.
Working all armhole decreases as set by back, dec 1 st at armhole edge of next 3 (3: 5: 5: 7: 7) rows, then on foll 3 alt rows, then on every foll 4th row until 28 (29: 29: 30: 30: 31) sts rem.
Work even until 9 (11: 11: 11: 11: 11) rows less

have been worked than on back to start of shoulder shaping, ending with a RS row.

Shape neck
Bind off 6 (6: 6: 6: 7: 7) sts at beg of next row. 22 (23: 23: 24: 23: 24) sts.
Dec 1 st at neck edge of next 4 rows, then on foll 2 (3: 3: 3: 3: 3) alt rows, ending with a WS row. 16 (16: 16: 17: 16: 17) sts.

Shape shoulder
Bind off 5 (5: 5: 6: 5: 6) sts at beg of next and foll alt row.
Work 1 row.
Bind off rem 6 (6: 6: 5: 6: 5) sts.

RIGHT FRONT
Cast on 40 (42: 44: 46: 48: 50) sts using size 8 (5mm) needles.
Work in garter st for 6 rows, ending with a WS row.
Change to size 10 (6mm) needles.
Row 7 (RS): Knit.
Row 8: K4, P to end.
Rep last 2 rows 7 times more.
Complete to match left front, reversing shapings.

SLEEVES (both alike)
Cast on 43 (45: 45: 47: 49: 49) sts using size 8 (5mm) needles.
Work in garter st for 18 rows, ending with a WS row.
Change to size 10 (6mm) needles.
Beg with a K row, cont in St st, inc 1 st at each end of next and every foll 16th (16th: 12th: 12th: 12th: 10th) row to 53 (55: 53: 53: 55: 57) sts, then on every foll - (-: 14th: 14th: 14th: 12th) row until there are - (-: 57: 59: 61: 63) sts.
Work even until sleeve measures 17¼ (17¼: 17¼: 17¾: 17¾: 17¾)in/44 (44: 44: 45: 45: 45)cm, ending with a WS row.

Shape sleeve cap
Bind off 4 (5: 5: 6: 6: 7) sts at beg of next 2 rows. 45 (45: 47: 47: 49: 49) sts.
Working all decreases as set by armholes, dec 1 st at each end of next 5 rows, then on foll 3

alt rows, then on every foll 4th row until 23 (23: 25: 25: 27: 27) sts rem.
Work 1 row, ending with a WS row.
Dec 1 st at each end of next and foll 0 (0: 1: 1: 2: 2) alt rows, then on foll 3 rows, ending with a WS row.
Bind off rem 15 sts.

FINISHING
BLOCK as described on page 123.
Join both shoulder seams using backstitch, or mattress stitch if preferred.

Collar
With RS facing and using size 8 (5mm) needles, starting and ending at front opening edges, pick up and knit 18 (20: 20: 20: 21: 21) sts up right side of neck, 23 (25: 25: 25: 27: 27) sts from back, then 18 (20: 20: 20: 21: 21) sts down left side of neck. 59 (65: 65: 65: 69: 69) sts.
Work in garter st until collar measures 4¾in/12cm, ending with RS of body facing for next row.
Bind off knitwise (on WS of collar).

Front bands (both alike)
With RS facing and using size 8 (5mm) needles, pick up and knit 86 sts along front opening edge, between cast-on edge and collar pick-up row.
**Row 1 (WS): P2, *K2, P2, rep from * to end.
Row 2: K2, *P2, inc once in each of next 2 sts, rep from * to last 4 sts, P2, K2. 126 sts.
Row 3: P2, K2, *P4, K2, rep from * to last 2 sts, P2.
Row 4: K2, P2, *C4B, P2, rep from * to last 2 sts, K2.
Row 5: Rep row 3.
Row 6: K2, P2, *K4, P2, rep from * to last 2 sts, K2.
Rows 7 to 10: Rep row 3 to 6.
Rows 11 and 12: Rep rows 3 and 4.
Bind off in patt (on WS).**

Collar bands (both alike)
With RS of collar facing (WS of body) and using size 8 (5mm) needles, pick up and knit

18 sts along front opening edge, between bound-off edge and collar pick-up row.
Work as given for front bands from ** to **, noting that there will be 24 sts after row 2.
Join row-end edges of collar and front bands.
See page 124 for finishing instructions, setting in sleeves using the set-in method and leaving side seams open for first 22 rows. Fasten front opening edges with decorative pin or brooch.

BOBBLE-TRIM SWEATER

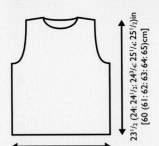

20¾ (21¾: 23: 24: 25: 26)in
[52.5 (55: 58: 60.5: 63: 65.5)cm]

23½ (24: 24½: 24¾: 25¼: 25½)in
[60 (61: 62: 63: 64: 65)cm]

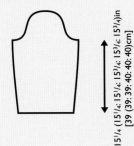

15¼ (15¼: 15¼: 15¾: 15¾: 15¾)in
[39 (39: 39: 40: 40: 40)cm]

SIZES

1	2	3	4	5	6	

TO FIT BUST

36	38	40	42	44	46	in
91	97	102	107	112	117	cm

YARN

Rowan Cotton Glace—oyster (730)

14	14	15	16	16	17 x 50g

NEEDLES AND CROCHET HOOK

1 pair size 2 (2¾mm) needles
1 pair size 3 (3¼mm) needles
Size C-2 (2.50mm) crochet hook

GAUGE

23 sts and 32 rows to 4in/10cm measured over St st using size 3 (3¼mm) needles.

CROCHET ABBREVIATIONS

sc = single crochet; ch = chain; sc2tog = (insert hook into next st, yarn over hook and draw loop through) twice, yarn over hook and draw through all 3 loops on hook.

BACK

Cast on 121 (127: 133: 139: 145: 151) sts using size 2 (2¾mm) needles.
Work in garter st for 6 rows, ending with a WS row.
Change to size 3 (3¼mm) needles.
Beg with a K row, cont in St st until back measures 14½ (15: 15: 15¼: 15½: 15¾)in/ 37 (38: 38: 39: 39: 40)cm, ending with a WS row.

Shape armholes

Bind off 6 (7: 7: 8: 8: 9) sts at beg of next 2 rows. 109 (113: 119: 123: 129: 133) sts.
Next row (RS): K3, K2tog, K to last 5 sts, K2tog tbl, K3.
Next row: P3, P2tog tbl, P to last 5 sts, P2tog, P3.
Working all armhole decreases as set by last 2 rows, dec 1 st at each end of next 3 (3: 5: 5: 7: 7) rows, then on foll 4 (5: 5: 6: 6: 7) alt rows,

then on every foll 4th row until 87 (89: 91: 93: 95: 97) sts rem.
Work even until armhole measures 9 (9: 9½: 9½: 9¾: 9¾)in/23 (23: 24: 24: 25: 25)cm, ending with a WS row.

Shape shoulders and back neck

Bind off 5 (5: 5: 6: 6: 6) sts at beg of next 2 rows. 77 (79: 81: 81: 83: 85) sts.
Next row (RS): Bind off 5 (5: 5: 6: 6: 6) sts, K until there are 9 (9: 10: 9: 9: 10) sts on right needle and turn, leaving rem sts on a holder. Work each side of neck separately.
Bind off 4 sts at beg of next row.
Bind off rem 5 (5: 6: 5: 5: 6) sts.
With RS facing, rejoin yarn to rem sts, bind off center 49 (51: 51: 51: 53: 53) sts, K to end.
Complete to match first side, reversing shapings.

FRONT

Work as given for back until 16 (18: 18: 18: 18: 18) rows less have been worked than on back to start of shoulder shaping, ending with a WS row.

Shape neck

Next row (RS): K29 (30: 31: 32: 32: 33) and turn, leaving rem sts on a holder.
Work each side of neck separately.
Bind off 5 sts at beg of next row. 24 (25: 26: 27: 27: 28) sts.
Dec 1 st at neck edge of next 4 rows, then on foll 5 (6: 6: 6: 6: 6) alt rows, ending with a WS row. 15 (15: 16: 17: 17: 18) sts.

Shape shoulder

Bind off 5 (5: 5: 6: 6: 6) sts at beg of next and foll alt row.
Work 1 row.
Bind off rem 5 (5: 6: 5: 5: 6) sts.
With RS facing, rejoin yarn to rem sts, bind off center 29 (29: 29: 29: 31: 31) sts, K to end.
Complete to match first side, reversing shapings.

SLEEVES (both alike)

Cast on 67 (69: 69: 71: 73: 73) sts using size 2 (2¾mm) needles.

Work in garter st for 6 rows, ending with a WS row.

Change to size 3 (3¼mm) needles.

Beg with a K row, cont in St st, shaping sides by inc 1 st at each end of 5th and every foll 12th (12th: 10th: 10th: 10th: 10th) row to 83 (85: 81: 79: 81: 93) sts, then on every foll 14th (14th: 12th: 12th: 12th: 12th) row until there are 85 (87: 89: 91: 93: 95) sts.

Work even until sleeve measures 15¼ (15¼: 15¼: 15¾: 15¾: 15¾)in/39 (39: 39: 40: 40: 40)cm, ending with a WS row.

Shape sleeve cap

Bind off 6 (7: 7: 8: 8: 9) sts at beg of next 2 rows. 73 (73: 75: 75: 77: 77) sts.

Working all decreases as set by back and front armholes, dec 1 st at each end of next 7 rows, then on foll 5 alt rows, then on every foll 4th row until 39 (39: 41: 41: 43: 43) sts rem.

Work 1 row, ending with a WS row.

Dec 1 st at each end of next and every foll alt row to 33 sts, then on foll 5 rows, ending with a WS row.

Bind off rem 23 sts.

FINISHING

BLOCK as described on page 123.

Join right shoulder seam using backstitch.

Neckband

With RS facing and using size 2 (2¾mm) needles, pick up and knit 20 (22: 22: 22: 22: 22) sts down left side of neck, 29 (29: 29: 29: 31: 31) sts from front, 20 (22: 22: 22: 22: 22) sts up right side of neck, then 57 (59: 59: 59: 61: 61) sts from back. 126 (132: 132: 132: 136: 136) sts.

Work in garter st for 2 rows, ending with a RS row.

Bind off knitwise (on WS).

See page 124 for finishing instructions, setting in sleeves using the set-in method.

Bobbles

With size C-2 (2.50mm) crochet hook, make a slip knot.

Round 1 (RS): 8sc in center of slip knot, 1 slip st in first sc.

Pull firmly on loose end of slip knot to close base of bobble.

Round 2: Ch1 (does NOT count as st), 2sc in each sc to end, 1 slip st in first sc. 16 sts.

Round 3: Ch1 (does NOT count as st), 1sc in each sc to end, 1 slip st in first sc.

Round 4: Ch1 (does NOT count as st), (sc2tog over next 2sc) 8 times, 1 slip st in first sc2tog. 8 sts.

Fasten off, leaving a fairly long end. Insert a little toy stuffing into bobble and run a gathering thread around top of last row. Pull up tight and fasten off securely.

Make 62 (64: 66: 70: 72: 74) bobbles in total.

Edging

**With size C-2 (2.50mm) crochet hook and RS facing, rejoin yarn at base of one side seam and cont as foll:

Round 1 (RS): Ch1 (does NOT count as st), 1sc in first cast-on st, *ch10, 1sc in top of bobble, ch10, skip 11 cast-on sts, 1sc in next st, rep from * to end, replacing sc at end of last rep with 1 slip st in first sc.

Fasten off.

Beg at other side seam, rep from ** once more, working sc into sts midway between sts used for first round.

Work edging around cast-on edge of sleeves in same way.

TASSEL-TRIM SWEATER

19³/₄ (21: 22: 23: 24: 25¹/₂)in
[50 (53: 55.5: 58.5: 61.5: 64.5)cm]

24¹/₂ (24³/₄: 25¹/₄: 25¹/₂: 26: 26¹/₂)in
[62 (63: 64: 65: 66: 67)cm]

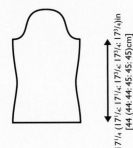

17¹/₄ (17¹/₄: 17¹/₄: 17³/₄: 17³/₄: 17³/₄)in
[44 (44: 44: 45: 45: 45)cm]

SIZES

1	2	3	4	5	6

TO FIT BUST

36	38	40	42	44	46	in
91	97	102	107	112	117	cm

YARN

Rowan Calmer—cream (460)

8	8	9	9	10	10 x 50g

NEEDLES

1 pair size 6 (4mm) needles
1 pair size 8 (5mm) needles
2 double-pointed size 6 (4mm) needles

GAUGE

21 sts and 30 rows to 4in/10cm measured over St st using size 8 (5mm) needles.

SPECIAL ABBREVIATION

tassel 3 = holding WS of tassel against RS of main section, K tog first st of tassel with next st of main section, K tog next 2 sts of tassel with next 2 sts of main section in same way.

TASSELS

Cast on 3 sts using double-pointed size 6 (4mm) needles.
Row 1 (RS): K3, *without turning slip these 3 sts to opposite end of needle and bring yarn to opposite end of work pulling it quite tightly across WS of work, K these 3 sts again, rep from * until tassel is 2in/5cm long.
Break yarn and leave sts on a holder.
Make required number of tassels in this way—you will need 36 (44: 44: 44: 52: 52) for back, same number for front, and 28 for each sleeve.

BACK

Cast on 105 (111: 117: 123: 129: 135) sts using size 6 (4mm) needles. Work in garter st for 4 rows, ending with a WS row.
Row 5 (RS): K11 (4: 7: 10: 3: 6), tassel 3, *K7, tassel 3, rep from * to last 11 (4: 7: 10: 3: 6) sts, K to end.

Row 6: Knit.
Change to size 8 (5mm) needles.
Beg with a K row, work in St st for 8 rows, ending with a WS row.
Last 10 rows form tassel patt.
Using size 8 (5mm) needles throughout, work a further 22 rows in tassel patt, ending with a WS row. (4 rows of tassels completed.)
Beg with a K row, cont in St st, dec 1 st at each end of next and every foll 12th row until 97 (103: 109: 115: 121: 127) sts rem.
Work 9 rows, ending with a WS row.
Inc 1 st at each end of next and every foll 10th row until there are 105 (111: 117: 123: 129: 135) sts.
Work even until back measures 15¹/₂ (15³/₄: 15³/₄: 16: 16¹/₄: 16³/₄)in/39 (40: 40: 41: 41: 42)cm, ending with a WS row.
Shape armholes
Bind off 5 (6: 6: 7: 7: 8) sts at beg of next 2 rows. 95 (99: 105: 109: 115: 119) sts.
Dec 1 st at each end of next 5 (5: 7: 7: 9: 9) rows, then on foll 2 (3: 3: 4: 4: 5) alt rows, then on every foll 4th row until 77 (79: 81: 83: 85: 87) sts rem.
Work even until armhole measures 9 (9: 9¹/₂: 9¹/₂: 9³/₄: 9³/₄)in/23 (23: 24: 24: 25: 25)cm, ending with a WS row.
Shape shoulders and back neck
Bind off 5 (5: 6: 6: 6: 6) sts at beg of next 2 rows. 67 (69: 69: 71: 73: 75) sts.
Next row (RS): Bind off 5 (5: 6: 6: 6: 6) sts, K until there are 10 (10: 9: 10: 10: 11) sts on right needle and turn, leaving rem sts on a holder.
Work each side of neck separately.
Bind off 4 sts at beg of next row.
Bind off rem 6 (6: 5: 6: 6: 7) sts.
With RS facing, rejoin yarn to rem sts, bind off center 37 (39: 39: 39: 41: 41) sts, K to end.
Complete to match first side, reversing shapings.

FRONT

Work as given for back until 12 (14: 14: 14: 14: 14) rows less have been worked than on back to start of shoulder shaping, ending with a WS row.

Shape neck

Next row (RS): K28 (29: 30: 31: 31: 32) and turn, leaving rem sts on a holder.

Work each side of neck separately.

Bind off 5 sts at beg of next row. 23 (24: 25: 26: 26: 27) sts.

Dec 1 st at neck edge of next 5 rows, then on foll 2 (3: 3: 3: 3: 3) alt rows. 16 (16: 17: 18: 18: 19) sts.

Work 1 row, ending with a WS row.

Shape shoulder

Bind off 5 (5: 6: 6: 6: 6) sts at beg of next and foll alt row.

Work 1 row.

Bind off rem 6 (6: 5: 6: 6: 7) sts.

With RS facing, rejoin yarn to rem sts, bind off center 21 (21: 21: 21: 23: 23) sts, K to end.

Complete to match first side, reversing shapings.

SLEEVES (both alike)

Cast on 79 (81: 81: 83: 85: 85) sts using size 6 (4mm) needles.

Work in garter st for 4 rows, ending with a WS row.

Row 5 (RS): K8 (9: 9: 10: 11: 11), tassel 3, *K7, tassel 3, rep from * to last 8 (9: 9: 10: 11: 11) sts, K to end.

Row 6: Knit.

Change to size 8 (5mm) needles.

Beg with a K row, work in St st for 8 rows, dec 1 st at each end of 7th of these rows and ending with a WS row. 77 (79: 79: 81: 83: 83) sts.

Last 10 rows form tassel patt and start sleeve shaping.

Using size 8 (5mm) needles throughout, work a further 22 rows in tassel patt **and at same time** dec 1 st at each end of 5th and every foll 6th row, ending with a WS row. (4 rows of tassels completed.) 71 (73: 73: 75: 77: 77) sts.

Beg with a K row, cont in St st, dec 1 st at each end of next and every foll 6th row to 65 (67: 67: 69: 71: 71) sts, then on every foll 8th

row until 61 (63: 63: 65: 67: 67) sts rem.

Work 11 rows, ending with a WS row.

Inc 1 st at each end of next and every foll 6th (6th: 4th: 4th: 4th: 4th) row to 77 (79: 71: 71: 73: 79) sts, then on every foll - (-: 6th: 6th: 6th: 6th) row until there are - (-: 81: 83: 85: 87) sts.

Work even until sleeve measures 17¼ (17¼: 17¼: 17¾: 17¾: 17¾)in/44 (44: 44: 45: 45: 45)cm, ending with a WS row.

Shape sleeve cap

Keeping patt correct, bind off 5 (6: 6: 7: 7: 8) sts at beg of next 2 rows. 67 (67: 69: 69: 71: 71) sts.

Dec 1 st at each end of next 7 rows, then on foll 3 alt rows, then on every foll 4th row until 39 (39: 41: 41: 43: 43) sts rem.

Work 1 row, ending with a WS row.

Dec 1 st at each end of next and every foll alt row to 27 sts, then on foll 3 rows, ending with a WS row.

Bind off rem 21 sts.

FINISHING

BLOCK as described on page 123.

Join right shoulder seam using backstitch, or mattress stitch if preferred.

Neckband

With RS facing and using size 6 (4mm) needles, pick up and knit 18 (20: 20: 20: 20: 20) sts down left side of neck, 21 (21: 21: 21: 23: 23) sts from front, 18 (20: 20: 20: 20: 20) sts up right side of neck, then 45 (47: 47: 47: 49: 49) sts from back. 102 (108: 108: 108: 112: 112) sts.

Work in garter st for 2 rows.

Bind off knitwise (on WS).

See page 124 for finishing instructions, setting in sleeves using the set-in method.

CABLE-TRIM SWEATER

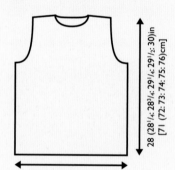

28 (28¼: 28¾: 29¼: 29½: 30)in
[71 (72: 73: 74: 75:76)cm]

22½ (23½: 24½: 25½: 26½: 27½)in
[57 (60: 62: 65: 67: 70)cm]

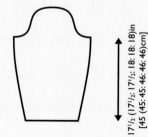

17½ (17½: 17½: 18: 18: 18)in
[45 (45: 45: 46: 46: 46)cm]

SIZES

1	2	3	4	5	6

TO FIT BUST

36	38	40	42	44	46	in
91	97	102	107	112	117	cm

YARN

Rowan Denim—ecru (324)

16	17	18	19	20	21 x 50g

NEEDLES

1 pair size 3 (3¼mm) needles
1 pair size 6 (4mm) needles
Cable needle

GAUGE

Before washing: 20 sts and 28 rows to 4in/10cm measured over St st using size 6 (4mm) needles.

Gauge note: Denim will shrink in length when washed for the first time. Allowances have been made in the pattern for shrinkage (see size diagram on the left for after-washing measurements).

SPECIAL ABBREVIATIONS

CB4 = slip next 2 sts onto cable needle and leave at back of work, K2, then K2 from cable needle.

C4F = slip next 2 sts onto cable needle and leave at front of work, K2, then K2 from cable needle.

BACK

Cast on 144 (150: 158: 164: 172: 178) sts using size 3 (3¼mm) needles.

Row 1 (RS): (P2, K2) 3 (2: 3: 2: 3: 2) times, *P2, K4, (P2, K2) twice, rep from * to last 6 (2: 6: 2: 6: 2) sts, P2, (K2, P2) 1 (0: 1: 0: 1: 0) times.

Row 2 and every foll alt row: (K2, P2) 3 (2: 3: 2: 3: 2) times, *K2, P4, (K2, P2) twice, rep from * to last 6 (2: 6: 2: 6: 2) sts, K2, (P2, K2) 1 (0: 1: 0: 1: 0) times.

Row 3: (P2, K2) 3 (2: 3: 2: 3: 2) times, *P2,

C4B, (P2, K2) twice, rep from * to last 6 (2: 6: 2: 6: 2) sts, P2, (K2, P2) 1 (0: 1: 0: 1: 0) times.

Row 5: Rep row 1.

Row 7: (P2, K2) 3 (2: 3: 2: 3: 2) times, *P2, C4F, (P2, K2) twice, rep from * to last 6 (2: 6: 2: 6: 2) sts, P2, (K2, P2) 1 (0: 1: 0: 1: 0) times.

Row 8: Rep row 2.

These 8 rows form fancy rib.

Cont in fancy rib for a further 31 rows, ending with a RS row.

Row 40 (dec) (WS): Rib 4 (0: 2: 5: 0: 3), *rib 1 (2: 1: 1: 1: 1), work 2 tog, rib 3, work 2 tog, rib 1, rep from * to last 5 (0: 3: 6: 1: 4) sts, rib 5 (0: 3: 6: 1: 4). 114 (120: 124: 130: 134: 140) sts. Change to size 6 (4mm) needles.

Beg with a K row, cont in St st until back measures 22 (22¼: 22½: 23: 23: 23¼)in/56 (57: 57: 58.5: 58.5: 59.5)cm, ending with a WS row.

Shape armholes

Bind off 6 (7: 7: 8: 8: 9) sts at beg of next 2 rows. 102 (106: 110: 114: 118: 122) sts.

Dec 1 st at each end of next 5 (5: 7: 7: 9: 9) rows, then on foll 5 (6: 5: 6: 5: 6) alt rows, then on every foll 4th row until 78 (80: 82: 84: 86: 88) sts rem.

Work even until armhole measures 10¾ (10¾: 11: 11: 11½: 11½)in/27 (27: 28: 28: 29: 29)cm, ending with a WS row.

Shape shoulders and back neck

Bind off 7 (7: 8: 8: 8: 8) sts at beg of next 2 rows. 64 (66: 66: 68: 70: 72) sts.

Next row (RS): Bind off 7 (7: 8: 8: 8: 8) sts, K until there are 12 (12: 11: 11: 12: 13) sts on right needle and turn, leaving rem sts on a holder.

Work each side of neck separately.

Bind off 4 sts at beg of next row.

Bind off rem 8 (8: 7: 8: 8: 9) sts.

With RS facing, rejoin yarn to rem sts, bind off center 26 (28: 28: 28: 30: 30) sts, K to end.

Complete to match first side, reversing shapings.

FRONT

Work as given for back until 16 (18: 18: 18: 18: 18) rows less have been worked than on back to start of shoulder shaping, ending with a WS row.

Shape neck

Next row (RS): K31 (32: 33: 34: 34: 35) and turn, leaving rem sts on a holder.

Work each side of neck separately.

Dec 1 st at neck edge of next 5 rows, then on foll 3 (4: 4: 4: 4: 4) alt rows, then on foll 4th row, ending with a WS row. 22 (22: 23: 24: 24: 25) sts.

Shape shoulder

Bind off 7 (7: 8: 8: 8: 8) sts at beg of next and foll alt row.

Work 1 row.

Bind off rem 8 (8: 7: 8: 8: 9) sts.

With RS facing, rejoin yarn to rem sts, bind off center 16 (16: 16: 16: 18: 18) sts, K to end.

Complete to match first side, reversing shapings.

SLEEVES (both alike)

Cast on 58 (60: 60: 62: 64: 64) sts using size 3 (3¼mm) needles.

Row 1 (RS): K0 (0: 0: 1: 2: 2), P1 (2: 2: 2: 2: 2), (K2, P2) 3 times, *K4, (P2, K2) twice, P2, rep from * to last 3 (4: 4: 5: 6: 6) sts, K2, P1 (2: 2: 2: 2: 2), K0 (0: 0: 1: 2: 2).

Row 2 and every foll alt row: P0 (0: 0: 1: 2: 2), K1 (2: 2: 2: 2: 2), (P2, K2) 3 times, *P4, (K2, P2) twice, K2, rep from * to last 3 (4: 4: 5: 6: 6) sts, P2, K1 (2: 2: 2: 2: 2), P0 (0: 0: 1: 2: 2).

Row 3: K0 (0: 0: 1: 2: 2), P1 (2: 2: 2: 2: 2), (K2, P2) 3 times, *C4B, (P2, K2) twice, P2, rep from * to last 3 (4: 4: 5: 6: 6) sts, K2, P1 (2: 2: 2: 2: 2), K0 (0: 0: 1: 2: 2).

Row 5: Rep row 1.

Row 7: K0 (0: 0: 1: 2: 2), P1 (2: 2: 2: 2: 2), (K2, P2) 3 times, *C4F, (P2, K2) twice, P2, rep from * to last 3 (4: 4: 5: 6: 6) sts, K2, P1 (2: 2: 2: 2: 2), K0 (0: 0: 1: 2: 2).

Row 8: Rep row 2.

These 8 rows form fancy rib.

Cont in fancy rib for a further 15 rows, ending with a RS row.

Row 24 (dec) (WS): Rib 1 (2: 2: 3: 4: 4), work 2 tog, *rib 3, work 2 tog, rep from * to

last 0 (1: 1: 2: 3: 3) sts, rib 0 (1: 1: 2: 3: 3). 46 (48: 48: 50: 52: 52) sts.

Change to size 6 (4mm) needles.

Beg with a K row, cont in St st, inc 1 st at each end of next and every foll 6th row to 58 (60: 68: 68: 70: 78) sts, then on every foll 8th row until there are 78 (80: 82: 84: 86: 88) sts.

Work even until sleeve measures 20¾ (20¾: 20¾: 21: 21: 21)in/52.5 (52.5: 52.5: 53.5: 53.5: 53.5)cm, ending with a WS row.

Shape sleeve cap

Bind off 6 (7: 7: 8: 8: 9) sts at beg of next 2 rows. 66 (66: 68: 68: 70: 70) sts.

Dec 1 st at each end of next 7 rows, then on foll 5 alt rows, then on every foll 4th row until 30 (30: 32: 32: 34: 34) sts rem.

Work 1 row, ending with a WS row.

Dec 1 st at each end of next and every foll alt row to 26 sts, then on foll 3 rows, ending with a WS row.

Bind off rem 20 sts.

FINISHING

Do NOT press.

Join right shoulder seam using backstitch.

Collar

With RS facing and using size 3 (3¼mm) needles, pick up and knit 24 (24: 24: 24: 27: 27) sts down left side of neck, 16 (16: 16: 16: 20: 20) sts from front, 24 (24: 24: 24: 27: 27) sts up right side of neck, then 36 (36: 36: 36: 40: 40) sts from back. 100 (100: 100: 100: 114: 114) sts.

Row 1 (RS of collar, WS of body): P2, *K2, P2, K4, P2, K2, P2, rep from * to end.

Row 2 and every foll alt row: K2, *P2, K2, P4, K2, P2, K2, rep from * to end.

Row 3: P2, *K2, P2, C4B, P2, K2, P2, rep from * to end.

Row 5: Rep row 1.

Row 7: P2, *K2, P2, C4F, P2, K2, P2, rep from * to end.

Row 8: Rep row 2.

These 8 rows form fancy rib.

Cont in fancy rib until collar measures 2¾in/7cm.

Change to size 6 (4mm) needles.

Cont in fancy rib until collar measures 6in/15cm.

Bind off in rib.

Machine wash all pieces before completing sewing together.

See page 124 for finishing instructions, setting in sleeves using the set-in method.

MOTIF BAG

YARNS

Jaeger Extra Fine Merino DK

A charcoal (959)	1	x 50g
B oatmeal (936)	1	x 50g
C camel (938)	1	x 50g
D gray tweed (978)	1	x 50g

CROCHET HOOK

Size E-4 (3.50mm) crochet hook

EXTRAS—12in/30cm by 24in/60cm piece of fabric for lining

GAUGE

Basic motif measures 3⅛in/8cm square using size E-4 (3.50mm) hook.

FINISHED SIZE

Completed bag measures 9½in/24cm wide and 10¼in/26cm deep.

CROCHET ABBREVIATIONS

ch = chain; **sc** = single crochet; **dc** = double crochet; **sp(s)** = space(es); **tr3tog** = *(yo) twice and insert hook as indicated, yo and draw loop through, (yo and draw through 2 loops on hook) twice, rep from * twice more, yo and draw through all 4 loops on hook; **tr4tog** = *(yo) twice and insert hook as

indicated, yo and draw loop through, (yo and draw through 2 loops on hook) twice, rep from * 3 times more, yo and draw through all 5 loops on hook; **yo** = yarn over hook.

BASIC MOTIF

Ch6 using size E-4 (3.50mm) hook and join with a slip st in first ch to form a ring.
Round 1 (WS): Ch4 (counts as 1dc and 1ch), (1dc in ring, ch1) 7 times, 1 slip st in 3rd of 4ch at beg of round.
Round 2: 1 slip st in first ch sp, ch4 (does NOT count as st), tr3tog in same ch sp, (ch4, tr4tog in next ch sp) 7 times, ch4, 1 slip st in top of tr3tog at beg of round.
Round 3: Ch1 (does NOT count as st), 1sc in same place as slip st at end of previous round, *ch4, 1dc in next ch sp, ch4, 1sc in next tr4tog, ch4, skip 4ch**, 1sc in next tr4tog, rep from * to end, ending last rep at **, 1 slip st in first sc.
Round 4: Ch1 (does NOT count as st), 1sc in same place as slip st at end of previous round, *4sc in next ch sp, 3sc in next dc**, (4sc in next ch sp, 1sc in next sc) twice, rep from * to end, ending last rep at **, 4sc in next ch sp, 1sc in next sc, 4sc in next ch sp, 1 slip st in first sc.
Fasten off.
Basic motif is a square. In each corner there are 3sc and between these corner sc there are a further 14sc.

BAG

Make 18 basic motifs in total—6 in yarn A, 3 in yarn B, 4 in yarn C, and 5 in yarn D.
Foll diagram, join motifs to form a strip 6 motifs wide and 3 motifs deep by sewing (or crocheting) motifs together along side of central 10sc along joining edges. Join ends of strip to form a tube in same way, then join base seam in same way.

Edging

With RS facing, using size E-4 (3.50mm) hook and yarn A, join yarn along one edge of one of top opening edge motifs, joining yarn to 3rd sc

after the corner sc, and cont as foll:
Edging round (RS): Ch1 (does NOT count as st), 1sc in same place as where yarn was joined, 1sc in each of next 9sc of same motif, *ch5**, skip 3 corner sc and foll 2sc of next motif, 1sc in each of next 10sc, rep from * to end, ending last rep at **, 1 slip st in first sc. 90 sts.
Next round: Ch1 (does NOT count as st), 1sc in each sc and 5sc in each ch sp to end, 1 slip st in first sc.
Next round: Ch1 (does NOT count as st), 1sc in each sc to end, 1 slip st in first sc.
Rep last round once more.
Fasten off.

HANDLES (make 2)

Ch65 using size E-4 (3.50mm) hook and yarn A.
Row 1: 1sc in 2nd ch from hook, 1sc in each sc to end, turn. 64 sts.
Row 2: Ch1 (does NOT count as st), 1sc in each sc to end, turn.
Rep row 2 twice more.
Fasten off.

FINISHING

BLOCK as described on page 123.
Attach ends of handles inside upper opening edge of bag, positioning ends of handles 4in/10cm apart.
Cut 2 pieces of fabric same size as finished bag, adding seam allowance along all edges. Join lining pieces along side and lower edges. Fold seam allowance to WS around upper edge. Slip lining inside bag and slip stitch in place around upper edge.

D	C	A	D	C	A
A	D	B	A	B	D
C	A	D	C	A	B

MOTIF SCARF

YARNS

Jaeger Extra Fine Merino DK

A charcoal (959)	2	x 50g
B oatmeal (936)	2	x 50g
C camel (938)	2	x 50g
D gray tweed (978)	2	x 50g

CROCHET HOOK

Size E-4 (3.50mm) crochet hook

GAUGE

Basic motif measures 3⅛in/8cm square using size E-4 (3.50mm) hook.

FINISHED SIZE

Completed scarf measures 10in/25cm wide and 69½in/177cm long.

CROCHET ABBREVIATIONS

Abbreviations as for motif bag (see page 88).

BASIC MOTIF

Make as for basic motif for motif bag (see page 88).

SCARF

Make 66 basic motifs in total—15 in yarn A, 17 in yarn B, 17 in yarn C, and 17 in yarn D. Foll diagram, join motifs to form a strip 22 motifs long and 3 motifs wide by sewing (or crocheting) motifs together along side of central 10sc along joining edges.

Edging

With RS facing, using size E-4 (3.50mm) hook and yarn A, join yarn along one long edge of joined motifs, joining yarn to 3rd sc after the corner sc, and cont as foll:

Edging round (RS): Ch1 (does NOT count as st), 1sc in same place as where yarn was joined, 1sc in each of next 9sc of same motif, *(ch5**, skip 3 corner sc and foll 2sc of next motif, 1sc in each of next 10sc) to end motif, ch5, skip 3 corner sc and foll 2sc of end motif, 1sc in each of next 13sc, 2sc in center sc of corner group of 3sc, 1sc in each of next 13sc, rep from * to end, ending last rep at **, 1 slip st in first sc.

Next round: Ch1 (does NOT count as st), 1sc in each sc and 5sc in each ch sp to end, 1 slip st in first sc.

Fasten off.

FINISHING

BLOCK as described on page 123.

C	A	B
A	B	D
D	C	A
B	D	C
C	A	B
B	C	D
D	B	A
A	D	C
C	B	A
A	D	C
B	C	D
A	D	B
B	C	A
A	B	D
B	C	A
C	D	B
D	A	C
C	B	D
A	D	C
D	C	B
B	A	D
D	C	B

BOBBLE-TRIM SCARF

YARN
Rowan Cotton Glace—oyster (730)
5 x 50g

NEEDLES AND CROCHET HOOK
1 pair size 2 (2¾mm) needles
Size C-2 (2.50mm) crochet hook

EXTRAS—washable toy stuffing

GAUGE
25 sts and 42 rows to 4in/10cm measured
over seed stitch using size 2 (2¾mm) needles.

FINISHED SIZE
Completed scarf measures 6½in/17cm wide
and 63in/160cm long, excluding bobble trim.

CROCHET ABBREVIATIONS
sc = single crochet; **ch** = chain; **sc2tog** =
(insert hook into next st, yarn over hook and
draw loop through) twice, yarn over hook
and draw through all 3 loops on hook.

SCARF
Cast on 43 sts using size 2 (2¾mm) needles.
Row 1 (RS): K1, *P1, K1, rep from * to end.
Row 2: Rep row 1.
These 2 rows form seed st.

Cont in seed st until scarf measures
63in/160cm, ending with a WS row.
Bind off in seed st.

FINISHING
BLOCK as described on page 123.
Bobbles (make 10)
With size C-2 (2.50mm) crochet hook, make a
slip knot.
Round 1 (RS): 8sc in center of slip knot,
1 slip st in first sc.
Pull firmly on loose end of slip loop to close
base of bobble.
Round 2: Ch1 (does NOT count as st), 2sc in
each sc to end, 1 slip st in first sc. 16 sts.
Round 3: Ch1 (does NOT count as st), 1sc
in each sc to end, 1 slip st in first sc.
Round 4: Ch1 (does NOT count as st),
(sc2tog over next 2sc) 8 times, 1 slip st in first
sc2tog. 8 sts.
Fasten off, leaving a fairly long end. Insert a
little toy stuffing into bobble and run a
gathering thread around top of last row. Pull
up tight and fasten off securely.
Edging
With size C-2 (2.50mm) crochet hook and RS
facing, rejoin yarn at beg of bound-off edge and
cont as foll:
Row 1 (RS): Ch1 (does NOT count as st),
1sc in first bound-off st, ch9, 1sc in top of
bobble, ch9, skip 12 bound-off sts, 1sc in each
of next 2 sts, ch9, 1sc in top of next bobble,
ch9, skip 13 bound-off sts, 1sc in each of next
2 sts, ch9, 1sc in top of next bobble, ch9, skip
12 bound-off sts, 1sc in last st, turn, 1 slip st in
each of next 6 bound-off sts, ch1, 1sc in same
st as last slip st, (ch9, 1sc in top of next
bobble, ch9, skip 14 bound-off sts, 1sc in next
st) twice.
Fasten off.
Work edging across cast-on edge in same way.

CABLED SCARF

These 12 rows form patt.
Cont in patt until scarf measures approx
79½in/202cm, ending after patt row 4.
Bind off in patt.

FINISHING
BLOCK as described on page 123.
Cut 13¾in/35cm lengths of yarn and knot
groups of 4 of these lengths through every
3rd st along cast-on and bound-off edges to
form fringe.

YARN
Rowan Calmer—ecru (461)
4 x 50g

NEEDLES
1 pair size 8 (5mm) needles
Cable needle

GAUGE
21 sts and 30 rows to 4in/10cm measured
over St st using size 8 (5mm) needles.

FINISHED SIZE
Completed scarf measures 6in/15cm wide and
79½in/202cm long, excluding fringe.

SPECIAL ABBREVIATION
C12B = slip next 6 sts onto cable needle
and leave at back of work, K6, then K6 from
cable needle.

SCARF
Cast on 57 sts using size 8 (5mm) needles.
Cont in patt as foll:
Row 1 (RS): K12, (P3, K12) 3 times.
Row 2: P12, (K1, yo, K2tog, P12) 3 times.
Row 3: C12B, (P3, C12B) 3 times.
Row 4: Rep row 2.
Rows 5 to 12: Rep rows 1 and 2, 4 times.

GARTER-RIB SWEATER

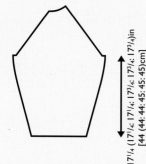

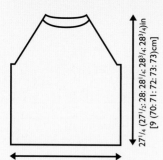

22 (23¹/₂: 24¹/₄: 25¹/₂: 26¹/₂: 27³/₄)in
[56 (59.5: 61.5: 65: 67: 70.5)cm]

27¹/₄ (27¹/₂: 28: 28¹/₄: 28³/₄: 28³/₄)in
[9 (70: 71: 72: 73: 73)cm]

17¹/₄ (17¹/₄: 17¹/₄: 17³/₄: 17³/₄: 17³/₄)in
[44 (44: 44: 45: 45: 45)cm]

SIZES

1	2	3	4	5	6

TO FIT BUST

36	38	40	42	44	46	in
91	97	102	107	112	117	cm

YARN

Rowan All Seasons Cotton—mocha
(212)

16	16	17	18	18	19 x 50g

NEEDLES

1 pair size 6 (4mm) needles
1 pair size 7 (4½mm) needles

GAUGE

18 sts and 25 rows to 4in/10cm measured
over St st using size 7 (4½mm) needles.

BACK

Cast on 101 (107: 111: 117: 121: 127) sts using
size 6 (4mm) needles.
Row 1 (WS): Purl.
Row 2: P2 (0: 2: 0: 2: 0), *K2, P3, rep from * to
last 4 (2: 4: 2: 4: 2) sts, K2, P2 (0: 2: 0: 2: 0).
These 2 rows form patt.
Work in patt for a further 3 rows, ending with
a WS row.
Change to size 7 (4½mm) needles.
Cont in patt until back measures 17in/43cm,
ending with a WS row.
Shape raglan armholes
Keeping patt correct, bind off 4 sts at beg of
next 2 rows. 93 (99: 103: 109: 113: 119) sts.
1st and 2nd sizes only
Dec 1 st at each end of next and foll 4th row.
87 (95: -: -: -: -) sts.
Work 3 (1: -: -: -: -) rows, ending with a WS row.
All sizes
Dec 1 st at each end of next 1 (1: 1: 5: 5: 9)
rows, then on every foll alt row until 37 (39:
39: 39: 41: 41) sts rem.
Work 1 row, ending with a WS row.
Shape back neck
Next row (RS): Work 2 tog, patt 3 sts and

turn, leaving rem sts on a holder.
Work each side of neck separately.
Dec 1 st at beg of next row.
Bind off rem 3 sts.
With RS facing, rejoin yarn to rem sts, bind off
center 27 (29: 29: 29: 31: 31) sts, patt to last 2
sts, work 2 tog. 4 sts.
Complete to match first side, reversing
shapings.

FRONT

Work as given for back until 47 (51: 51: 51: 53:
53) sts rem in raglan armhole shaping.
Work 1 row, ending with a WS row.
Shape neck
Next row (RS): Work 2 tog, patt 16 (18:
18: 18: 18: 18) sts and turn, leaving rem sts on
a holder.
Work each side of neck separately.
Bind off 5 sts at beg of next row. 12 (14: 14:
14: 14: 14) sts.
Dec 1 st at neck edge of next 5 rows, then on
foll 1 (2: 2: 2: 2: 2) alt rows **and at same
time** dec 1 st at raglan armhole edge of next
and every foll alt row. 2 sts.
Work 1 row, ending with a WS row.
Next row (RS): K2tog and fasten off.
With RS facing, rejoin yarn to rem sts, bind off
center 11 (11: 11: 11: 13: 13) sts, patt to last 2
sts, work 2 tog.
Complete to match first side, reversing
shapings.

SLEEVES

Cast on 47 (49: 49: 51: 53: 53) sts using size 6
(4mm) needles.
Row 1 (WS): Purl.
Row 2: P0 (1: 1: 2: 3: 3), *K2, P3, rep from * to
last 2 (3: 3: 4: 5: 5) sts, K2, P0 (1: 1: 2: 3: 3).
These 2 rows form patt.
Work in patt for a further 3 rows, ending with
a WS row.
Change to size 7 (4½mm) needles.
Cont in patt, shaping sides by inc 1 st at each
end of next and every foll 4th row to 69 (71:
77: 77: 79: 85) sts, then on every foll 6th row

until there are 87 (89: 91: 93: 95: 97) sts, taking inc sts into patt.

Work even until sleeve measures 17¼ (17¼: 17¼: 17¾: 17¾: 17¾)in/44 (44: 44: 45: 45: 45)cm, ending with a WS row.

Shape raglan

Keeping patt correct, bind off 4 sts at beg of next 2 rows. 79 (81: 83: 85: 87: 89) sts.

Dec 1 st at each end of next and every foll alt row until 19 sts rem.

Work 1 row, ending with a WS row.

Left sleeve only

Dec 1 st at each end of next row, then bind off 4 sts at beg of foll row. 13 sts.

Dec 1 st at beg of next row, then bind off 6 sts at beg of foll row.

Right sleeve only

Bind off 5 sts at beg and dec 1 st at end of next row. 13 sts.

Work 1 row.

Bind off 6 sts at beg and dec 1 st at end of next row.

Work 1 row.

Both sleeves

Bind off rem 6 sts.

FINISHING

BLOCK as described on page 123.

Join both front and right back raglan seams using backstitch, or mattress stitch if preferred.

Collar

With RS facing and using size 6 (4mm) needles, pick up and knit 12 sts from left sleeve, 11 (15: 15: 15: 15: 15) sts down left side of neck, 13 (13: 13: 13: 16: 16) sts from front, 11 (15: 15: 15: 15: 15) sts up right side of neck, 12 sts from right sleeve, then 33 (35: 35: 35: 37: 37) sts from back. 92 (102: 102: 102: 107: 107) sts.

Row 1 (WS of body, RS of collar): K2, *P3, K2, rep from * to end.

Row 2: Purl.

These 2 rows form patt.

Cont in rib until collar measures 4in/10cm, ending with a WS row.

Change to size 7 (4½mm) needles.

Cont in patt until collar measures 7¾in/20cm.

Bind off in patt.

See page 124 for finishing instructions, reversing collar seam for turn-back.

TWEED PONCHO

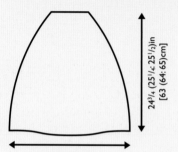

24¾ (25¼: 25½)in
[63 (64: 65)cm]

49 (51¼: 53¼)in
[124.5 (130: 135.5)cm]

SIZES

1–2	3–4	5–6	

TO FIT BUST

36–38	40–42	44–46	in
91–97	102–107	112–117	cm

YARN

Rowan Plaid—brown tweed (166)

10	11	12	x 100g

NEEDLES

1 pair size 11 (8mm) needles

GAUGE

11 sts and 15 rows to 4in/10cm measured over St st using size 11 (8mm) needles.

BACK AND FRONT (both alike)

Cast on 137 (143: 149) sts using size 11 (8mm) needles.
Work in garter st for 2 rows, ending with a WS row.
Beg with a K row, work in St st for 14 rows, ending with a WS row.
Place markers on 32nd (33rd: 34th) sts in from both ends of last row.
Row 17 (RS): (K to within 2 sts of marked st, K2tog tbl, K marked st, K2tog) twice, K to end.
Row 18: Purl.
Rep rows 17 and 18, 17 (18: 19) times. 65 (67: 69) sts.
Next row (RS): Rep row 17.
Next row: Purl.
Next row: Knit.
Next row: Purl.
Rep last 4 rows 9 times more. 25 (27: 29) sts.
Rep rows 17 and 18 once.
Break yarn and leave rem 21 (23: 25) sts on a holder.

FINISHING

BLOCK as described on page 123.
Join right shoulder and side seam using backstitch, or mattress stitch if preferred.

Collar

With RS facing and using size 11 (8mm) needles, K 21 (23: 25) sts of front, then K 21 (23: 25) sts of back. 42 (46: 50) sts.
Next row (WS): K2, *P2, K2, rep from * to end.
Next row: P2, *K2, P2, rep from * to end.
Rep last 2 rows until collar measures 4in/10cm, ending with a WS row.
Next row (RS): P2, *K1, M1, K1, P2, rep from * to end. 52 (57: 62) sts.
Next row: K2, *P3, K2, rep from * to end.
Next row: P2, *K3, P2, rep from * to end.
Rep last 2 rows until collar measures 8¾in/22cm.
Bind off in rib.
See page 124 for finishing instructions, reversing collar seam for turn-back.
Cut 10in/25cm lengths of yarn and knot groups of 3 of these lengths through every st of cast-on and bound-off edges to form fringe.

ZIGZAG SCARF

YARNS
Rowan 4 ply Soft
A	taupe (386)	3	x 50g
B	off-white (376)	3	x 50g
C	expresso (389)	2	x 50g
D	light dusty plum (378)	2	x 50g

NEEDLES
1 pair size 2 (2¾mm) needles
1 pair size 3 (3¼mm) needles

GAUGE
35 sts and 38 rows to 4in/10cm measured over pattern using size 3 (3¼mm) needles.

FINISHED SIZE
Completed scarf measures 10in/26cm wide and approx 80½in/204cm long, excluding fringe at each end.

SCARF
First Section
Cast on 91 sts using size 2 (2¾mm) needles and yarn A.
Row 1 (RS): K1, *yo, K3, K3tog, K3, yo, K1, rep from * to end.
Row 2: Knit.
These 2 rows form patt.
Joining in and breaking off yarn as required,

cont in patt using colors as foll:
Rows 3 to 6: Using yarn A.
Change to size 3 (3¼mm) needles.
Rows 7 to 30: Using yarn A.
Rows 31 and 32: Using yarn B.
Rows 33 and 34: Using yarn A.
Rows 35 to 50: Rep rows 31 to 34 four times.
Rows 51 and 52: Using yarn B.
Rows 53 to 82: Using yarn C.
Rows 83 and 84: Using yarn B.
Rows 85 and 86: Using yarn A.
Rows 87 to 98: Rep rows 83 to 86 three times.
Rows 99 and 100: Using yarn B.
Rows 101 to 108: Using yarn C.
Rows 109 to 138: Using yarn D.
Rows 139 to 146: Using yarn C.
Rows 147 to 154: Using yarn D.
Rows 155 to 172: Using yarn C.
Rows 173 and 174: Using yarn A.
Rows 175 and 176: Using yarn B.
Rows 177 to 200: Rep rows 173 to 176 six times.
Rows 201 and 202: Using yarn A.
Rows 203 to 262: Using yarn B.
Rows 263 to 292: Using yarn A.
Rows 293 and 294: Using yarn B.
Rows 295 and 296: Using yarn A.
Rows 297 to 312: Rep rows 293 to 296 four times.
Rows 313 and 314: Using yarn B.
Rows 315 to 344: Using yarn C.
Rows 345 and 346: Using yarn B.
Rows 347 and 348: Using yarn A.
Rows 349 to 360: Rep rows 345 to 348 three times.
Rows 361 and 362: Using yarn B.
Rows 363 to 370: Using yarn C.
Rows 371 to 387: Using yarn D.**
Break yarn and leave sts on a holder.
Second section
Work as given for first section to **.
Join sections
Holding sections with RS facing, bind off both sets of sts together by taking one st from first section with corresponding st from second section.

FINISHING
BLOCK as described on page 123.
Cut 12½in/32cm lengths of yarn A and knot groups of 13 of these lengths through each point of cast-on edges to form fringe.

BEADED JACKET & TEXTURED JACKET

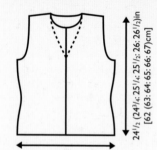

20¹/₂ (21¹/₂: 22¹/₂: 23¹/₂: 24¹/₂: 25¹/₂)in
[51.5 (54: 57: 59.5: 62.5: 65)cm]

24¹/₂ (24³/₄: 25¹/₄: 25¹/₂: 26: 26¹/₂)in
[62 (63: 64: 65: 66: 67)cm]

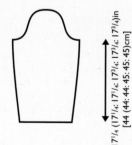

17¹/₄ (17¹/₄: 17¹/₄: 17³/₄: 17³/₄: 17³/₄)in
[44 (44: 44: 45: 45: 45)cm]

SIZES

1	2	3	4	5	6	

TO FIT BUST

36	38	40	42	44	46	in
91	97	102	107	112	117	cm

YARNS

Jaeger Extra Fine Merino DK
BEADED VERSION—camel (938)—see left

13	13	14	14	15	15 x 50g

TEXTURED VERSION—ash (976)—see page 20

13	13	14	14	15	15 x 50g

NEEDLES

1 pair size 3 (3mm) needles
1 pair size 5 (3¾mm) needles

BUTTONS—7 for beaded version, or 6 for textured version

BEADS—beaded version only: approx 1,060 (1,120: 1,180: 1,250: 1,310: 1,370) 2.5mm bronze-colored glass beads (Rowan J3000-01009)

GAUGE

22 sts and 30 rows to 4in/10cm measured over St st using size 5 (3¾mm) needles.

SPECIAL ABBREVIATION

bead 1 = place a bead by bringing yarn to RS of work and slipping bead up next to st just worked, slip next st purlwise from left needle to right needle and take yarn to WS of work, leaving bead sitting on RS of work in front of slipped st. Do not place beads on edge stitches of work as this will interfere with seams.

Pattern note: Before starting to knit beaded jacket, thread beads onto yarn. To do this, thread a fine sewing needle (one that will easily pass through the beads) with sewing thread. Knot ends of thread and then pass end of yarn through this loop. Thread a bead onto sewing thread and then gently slide it along and onto knitting yarn. Continue in this way until required number of beads are on yarn.

BACK

Cast on 113 (119: 125: 131: 137: 143) sts using size 3 (3mm) needles.
Row 1 (RS): K1 (0: 1: 0: 1: 0), *P1, K1, rep from * to last 0 (1: 0: 1: 0: 1) st, P0 (1: 0: 1: 0: 1).
Row 2: Rep row 1.
These 2 rows form seed st.
Cont in seed st for a further 8 rows, ending with a WS row.
Change to size 5 (3¾mm) needles.
Row 1 (RS): Knit.
Row 2 and every foll alt row: Purl.
Beaded version only
Row 3: K6 (9: 2: 5: 8: 1), *bead 1, K9, rep from * to last 7 (10: 3: 6: 9: 2) sts, bead 1, K6 (9: 2: 5: 8: 1).
Textured version only
Row 3: K6 (9: 2: 5: 8: 1), *P1, K9, rep from * to last 7 (10: 3: 6: 9: 2) sts, P1, K6 (9: 2: 5: 8: 1).
Both versions
Rows 5 and 7: Knit.
Beaded version only
Row 9: K1 (4: 7: 10: 3: 6), *bead 1, K9, rep from * to last 2 (5: 8: 11: 4: 7) sts, bead 1, K1 (4: 7: 10: 3: 6).
Textured version only
Row 9: K1 (4: 7: 10: 3: 6), *P1, K9, rep from * to last 2 (5: 8: 11: 4: 7) sts, P1, K1 (4: 7: 10: 3: 6).
Both versions
Row 11: Knit.
Row 12: Purl.
These 12 rows form patt.
Cont in patt, dec 1 st at each end of 15th (17th: 17th: 17th: 17th: 19th) and every foll 10th row to 107 (113: 119: 125: 131: 137) sts, then on every foll 8th row until there are 103 (109: 115: 121: 127: 133) sts.
Work 5 (7: 7: 7: 7: 9) rows, ending with a WS row.
Inc 1 st at each end of next and every foll 8th row until there are 113 (119: 125: 131: 137: 143) sts, taking inc sts into patt.

Work even until back measures 15½ (15¾: 15¾: 16: 16¼: 16¾)in/39 (40: 40: 41: 41: 42)cm, ending with a WS row.

Shape armholes

Keeping patt correct, bind off 5 (6: 6: 7: 7: 8) sts at beg of next 2 rows. 103 (107: 113: 117: 123: 127) sts.

Dec 1 st at each end of next 3 (3: 5: 5: 7: 7) rows, then on foll 3 (4: 4: 5: 5: 6) alt rows, then on every foll 4th row until 87 (89: 91: 93: 95: 97) sts rem.

Work even until armhole measures 9 (9: 9½: 9½: 9¾: 9¾)in/23 (23: 24: 24: 25: 25)cm, ending with a WS row.

Shape shoulders and back neck

Bind off 9 (9: 9: 9: 9: 10) sts at beg of next 2 rows. 69 (71: 73: 75: 77: 77) sts.

Next row (RS): Bind off 9 (9: 9: 9: 9: 10) sts, patt until there are 12 (12: 13: 14: 14: 13) sts on right needle and turn, leaving rem sts on a holder.

Work each side of neck separately.

Bind off 4 sts at beg of next row.

Bind off rem 8 (8: 9: 10: 10: 9) sts.

With RS facing, rejoin yarn to rem sts, cast off center 27 (29: 29: 29: 31: 31) sts, patt to end.

Complete to match first side, reversing shapings.

LEFT FRONT

Cast on 65 (68: 71: 74: 77: 80) sts using size 3 (3mm) needles.

Row 1 (RS): K1 (0: 1: 0: 1: 0), *P1, K1, rep from * to end.

Row 2: K1, *P1, K1, rep from * to last 0 (1: 0: 1: 0: 1) st, P0 (1: 0: 1: 0: 1).

These 2 rows form seed st.

Cont in seed st for a further 7 rows, ending with a RS row.

Row 10 (WS): Seed st 8 sts and slip these sts onto a holder, seed st to end. 57 (60: 63: 66: 69: 72) sts.

Change to size 5 (3¾mm) needles.

Row 1 (RS): Knit.

Row 2 and every foll alt row: Purl.

Beaded version only

Row 3: K6 (9: 2: 5: 8: 1), *bead 1, K9, rep from * to last st, K1.

Textured version only

Row 3: K6 (9: 2: 5: 8: 1), *P1, K9, rep from * to last st, K1.

Both versions

Rows 5 and 7: Knit.

Beaded version only

Row 9: K1 (4: 7: 10: 3: 6), *bead 1, K9, rep from * to last 6 sts, bead 1, K5.

Textured version only

Row 9: K1 (4: 7: 10: 3: 6), *P1, K9, rep from * to last 6 sts, P1, K5.

Both versions

Row 11: Knit.

Row 12: Purl.

These 12 rows form patt.

Cont in patt, dec 1 st at beg of 15th (17th: 17th: 17th: 17th: 19th) and every foll 10th row to 54 (57: 60: 63: 66: 69) sts, then on every foll 8th row until there are 52 (55: 58: 61: 64: 67) sts.

Work 5 (7: 7: 7: 7: 9) rows, ending with a WS row.

Inc 1 st at beg of next and every foll 8th row until there are 57 (60: 63: 66: 69: 72) sts, taking inc sts into patt.

Work even until left front matches back to beg of armhole shaping, ending with a WS row.

Shape armhole

Keeping patt correct, bind off 5 (6: 6: 7: 7: 8) sts at beg of next row. 52 (54: 57: 59: 62: 64) sts.

Work 1 row.

Beaded version only

Dec 1 st at armhole edge of next 3 (3: 5: 5: 7: 7) rows, then on foll 3 (4: 4: 5: 5: 6) alt rows, then on every foll 4th row until 44 (45: 46: 47: 48: 49) sts rem.

Work even until 15 (17: 17: 17: 17: 17) rows less have been worked than on back to start of shoulder shaping, ending with a RS row.

Shape neck

Keeping patt correct, bind off 9 (9: 9: 9: 10: 10) sts at beg of next row. 35 (36: 37: 38: 38: 39) sts.

Dec 1 st at neck edge of next 6 rows, then on foll 2 (3: 3: 3: 3: 3) alt rows, then on foll 4th row, ending with a WS row.

Textured version only

Dec 1 st at armhole edge of next 3 (3: 4: 4: 4: 4) rows. 49 (51: 53: 55: 58: 60) sts.

Work 1 (1: 0: 0: 0: 0) row, ending with a WS row.

Shape front slope

Dec 1 st at armhole edge of next 1 (1: 1: 1: 3: 3) rows, then on foll 2 (3: 4: 5: 5: 6) alt rows, then on 2 foll 4th rows **and at same time** dec 1 st at front slope edge on next and foll 6 (7: 8: 8: 8: 8) alt rows, then on foll 0 (0: 0: 0: 4th: 4th) row. 37 (37: 37: 38: 38: 39) sts.

Dec 1 st at front slope edge only on 2nd (2nd: 4th: 2nd: 4th: 2nd) and foll 0 (1: 0: 0: 0: 0) alt row, then on every foll 4th row until 26 (26: 27: 28: 28: 29) sts rem.

Work even until left front matches back to start of shoulder shaping, ending with a WS row.

Both versions

Shape shoulder

Bind off 9 (9: 9: 9: 9: 10) sts at beg of next and foll alt row. Work 1 row.

Bind off rem 8 (8: 9: 10: 10: 9) sts.

RIGHT FRONT

Cast on 65 (68: 71: 74: 77: 80) sts using size 3 (3mm) needles.

Row 1 (RS): K1, *P1, K1, rep from * to last 0 (1: 0: 1: 0: 1) st, P0 (1: 0: 1: 0: 1).

Row 2: K1 (0: 1: 0: 1: 0), *P1, K1, rep from * to end.

These 2 rows form seed st.

Cont in seed st for a further 2 rows, ending with a WS row.

Row 5 (RS): K1, P1, K1, P2tog, yo (to make a buttonhole), seed st to end.

Cont in seed st for a further 4 rows, ending with a RS row.

Row 10 (WS): Seed st to last 8 sts and turn, leaving rem 8 sts on a holder. 57 (60: 63: 66: 69: 72) sts.

Change to size 5 (3¾mm) needles.

Row 1 (RS): Knit.

Row 2 and every foll alt row: Purl.
Beaded version only
Row 3: K10, *bead 1, K9, rep from * to last 7 (10: 3: 6: 9: 2) sts, bead 1, K6 (9: 2: 5: 8: 1).
Textured version only
Row 3: K10, *P1, K9, rep from * to last 7 (10: 3: 6: 9: 2) sts, P1, K6 (9: 2: 5: 8: 1).
Both versions
Rows 5 and 7: Knit.
Beaded version only
Row 9: K5, *bead 1, K9, rep from * to last 2 (5: 8: 11: 4: 7) sts, bead 1, K1 (4: 7: 10: 3: 6).
Textured version only
Row 9: K5, *P1, K9, rep from * to last 2 (5: 8: 11: 4: 7) sts, P1, K1 (4: 7: 10: 3: 6).
Both versions
Row 11: Knit.
Row 12: Purl.
These 12 rows form patt.
Cont in patt, dec 1 st at end of 15th (17th: 17th: 17th: 17th: 19th) and every foll 10th row to 54 (57: 60: 63: 66: 69) sts, then on every foll 8th row until there are 52 (55: 58: 61: 64: 67) sts. Complete to match left front, reversing shapings.

SLEEVES (both alike)
Cast on 57 (59: 59: 61: 63: 63) sts using size 3 (3mm) needles.
Row 1 (RS): K1, *P1, K1, rep from * to end.
Row 2: Rep row 1.
These 2 rows form seed st.
Cont in seed st for a further 8 rows, ending with a WS row.
Change to size 5 (3¾mm) needles.
Row 1 (RS): Inc in first st, K to last st, inc in last st. 59 (61: 61: 63: 65: 65) sts.
Row 2 and every foll alt row: Purl.
Beaded version only
Row 3: K9 (10: 10: 1: 2: 2), *bead 1, K9, rep from * to last 10 (11: 11: 2: 3: 3) sts, bead 1, K9 (10: 10: 1: 2: 2).
Textured version only
Row 3: K9 (10: 10: 1: 2: 2), *P1, K9, rep from * to last 10 (11: 11: 2: 3: 3) sts, P1, K9 (10: 10: 1: 2: 2).

Both versions
Row 5: Knit.
Row 7: (Inc in first st) 0 (0: 1: 1: 1: 1) times, K to last 0 (0: 1: 1: 1: 1) st, (inc in last st) 0 (0: 1: 1: 1: 1) times. 59 (61: 63: 65: 67: 67) sts.
Beaded version only
Row 9: (Inc in first st) 1 (1: 0: 0: 0: 0) times, K3 (4: 6: 7: 8: 8), *bead 1, K9, rep from * to last 5 (6: 7: 8: 9: 9) sts, bead 1, K3 (4: 6: 7: 8: 8), (inc in last st) 1 (1: 0: 0: 0: 0) times. 61 (63: 63: 65: 67: 67) sts.
Textured version only
Row 9: (Inc in first st) 1 (1: 0: 0: 0: 0) times, K3 (4: 6: 7: 8: 8), *P1, K9, rep from * to last 5 (6: 7: 8: 9: 9) sts, P1, K3 (4: 6: 7: 8: 8), (inc in last st) 1 (1: 0: 0: 0: 0) times. 61 (63: 63: 65: 67: 67) sts.
Both versions
Row 11: Knit.
Row 12: Purl.
These 12 rows form patt and start sleeve shaping.
Cont in patt, inc 1 st at each end of 5th (5th: next: 3rd: 3rd: next) and every foll 8th (8th: 8th: 8th: 8th: 6th) row to 81 (83: 89: 91: 93: 75) sts, then on every foll 10th (10th: -: -: -: 8th) row until there are 85 (87: -: -: -: 95) sts, taking inc sts into patt.
Work even until sleeve measures 17¼ (17¼: 17¼: 17¾: 17¾: 17¾)in/44 (44: 44: 45: 45: 45)cm, ending with a WS row.
Shape sleeve cap
Keeping patt correct, bind off 5 (6: 6: 7: 7: 8) sts at beg of next 2 rows. 75 (75: 77: 77: 79: 79) sts.
Dec 1 st at each end of next 5 rows, then on foll 4 alt rows, then on every foll 4th row until 49 (49: 51: 51: 53: 53) sts rem.
Work 1 row, ending with a WS row.
Dec 1 st at each end of next and every foll alt row to 39 sts, then on foll 3 rows, ending with a WS row.
Bind off 5 sts at beg of next 2 rows.
Bind off rem 23 sts.

FINISHING
BLOCK as described on page 123.
Join both shoulder seams using backstitch.

Beaded version only
Left front band
Slip 8 sts from left front holder onto size 3 (3mm) needles and rejoin yarn with RS facing.
Cont in seed st as set until band, when slightly stretched, fits up left front opening edge to neck shaping, ending with a WS row.
Break yarn and leave sts on a holder.
Slip stitch band in place.
Mark positions for 7 buttons on this band section—first to come level with buttonhole already worked in right front, last to come just above neck shaping, and rem 5 buttons evenly spaced between.
Right front band
Slip 8 sts from right front holder onto size 3 (3mm) needles and rejoin yarn with WS facing.
Cont in seed st as set until band, when slightly stretched, fits up right front opening edge to neck shaping, ending with a WS row and with the addition of a further 5 buttonholes worked as foll:
Buttonhole row (RS): K1, P1, K1, P2tog, yo (to make a buttonhole), P1, K1, P1.
When band is complete, do NOT break off yarn.
Slip stitch band in place.
Collar
With RS facing and using size 3 (3mm) needles, seed st 8 sts from right front band, pick up and knit 21 (23: 23: 23: 24: 24) sts up right side of neck, 35 (37: 37: 37: 39: 39) sts from back, and 21 (23: 23: 23: 24: 24) sts down left side of neck, then seed st 8 sts from left front band. 93 (99: 99: 99: 103: 103) sts.
Work in seed st as set by bands for 3 rows, ending with a WS row.
Next row (RS of body): K1, P1, K1, P2tog, yo (to make 7th buttonhole), seed st to end.
Work in seed st for a further 4 rows.
Bind off 4 sts at beg of next 2 rows. 85 (91: 91: 91: 95: 95) sts.
Cont in seed st until collar measures 4¾in/12cm from pick-up row.
Bind off in seed st.

Textured version only

Place markers along front slope edges 3½in/9cm below shoulder seams.

Left front band and collar

Slip 8 sts from left front holder onto size 3 (3mm) needles and rejoin yarn with RS facing.

Cont in seed st as set until band, when slightly stretched, fits up left front opening edge to start of front slope shaping, ending with a WS row.

Shape for collar

Next row (RS of body, WS of collar section): Seed st 1 st, inc twice in next st (by working into front, back, and front again of st), seed st to end. 10 sts.

Work 5 rows.

Rep last 6 rows 6 times more. 22 sts.

Work even until collar section, unstretched, fits up front slope to marker, ending at outer (unshaped) edge.

Next row (RS of collar): Bind off 9 sts, turn and cast on 9 sts, turn and seed st to end. 22 sts.

Work even until collar section, unstretched, fits up rem section of front slope and across to center back neck, ending with a WS row. Bind off in seed st.

Slip stitch band and collar in place.

Mark positions for 6 buttons on this band section—first to come level with buttonhole already worked in right front, last to come ½in/1cm below start of front slope shaping, and rem 4 buttons evenly spaced between.

Right front band and collar

Slip 8 sts from right front holder onto size 3 (3mm) needles and rejoin yarn with WS facing.

Cont in seed st as set until right front band, when slightly stretched, fits up right front opening edge to start of front slope shaping, ending with a WS row and with the addition of a further 5 buttonholes worked as foll:

Buttonhole row (RS): K1, P1, K1, P2tog, yo (to make a buttonhole), P1, K1, P1.

Shape for collar

Next row (RS of body, WS of collar section): Seed st to last 2 sts, inc twice in next st, seed st 1 st. 10 sts.

Work 5 rows.

Rep last 6 rows 6 times more. 22 sts.

Work even until collar section, unstretched, fits up front slope to marker, ending at outer (unshaped) edge.

Next row (WS of collar): Bind off 9 sts, turn and cast on 9 sts, turn and seed st to end. 22 sts.

Work even until collar section, unstretched, fits up rem section of front slope and across to center back neck, ending with a WS row. Bind off in seed st.

Slip stitch band and collar in place, joining bound-off ends of collar sections.

Both versions

See page 124 for finishing instructions, setting in sleeves using the set-in method.

DIAMOND-PATTERN SWEATER

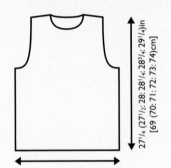

22¹/₂ (23¹/₄: 24¹/₂: 25¹/₄: 26¹/₂: 27¹/₄)in
[57 (59: 62: 64: 67: 69)cm]

27¹/₄ (27¹/₂: 28: 28¹/₄: 28¹/₄: 29¹/₄)in
[69 (70: 71: 72: 73: 74)cm]

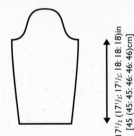

17¹/₂ (17¹/₂: 17¹/₂: 18: 18: 18)in
[45 (45: 45: 46: 46: 46)cm]

SIZES

| 1 | 2 | 3 | 4 | 5 | 6 |

TO FIT BUST

| 36 | 38 | 40 | 42 | 44 | 46 | in |
| 91 | 97 | 102 | 107 | 112 | 117 | cm |

YARN

Rowan 4 ply Soft—dark gray (372)

| 11 | 11 | 12 | 12 | 13 | 13 x 50g |

NEEDLES

1 pair size 2 (2³/₄mm) needles
1 pair size 3 (3¹/₄mm) needles

GAUGE

28 sts and 36 rows to 4in/10cm measured over St st using size 3 (3¹/₄mm) needles.

BACK

Cast on 159 (165: 173: 179: 187: 193) sts using size 2 (2³/₄mm) needles.
Row 1 (RS): (K1 tbl) 3 (3: 4: 4: 2: 2) times, *(P1 tbl) 3 times, (K1 tbl) 3 times, rep from * to last 0 (0: 1: 1: 5: 5) sts, (P1 tbl) 0 (0: 0: 0: 3: 3) times, (K1 tbl) 0 (0: 1: 1: 2: 2) times.
Row 2: (P1 tbl) 3 (3: 4: 4: 2: 2) times, *(K1 tbl) 3 times, (P1 tbl) 3 times, rep from * to last 0 (0: 1: 1: 5: 5) sts, (K1 tbl) 0 (0: 0: 0: 3: 3) times, (P1 tbl) 0 (0: 1: 1: 2: 2) times.
These 2 rows form twisted rib.
Cont in twisted rib for 5in/13cm, ending with a WS row.
Change to size 3 (3¹/₄mm) needles.
Beg and ending rows as indicated and rep the 36 row patt rep throughout, cont in patt from chart until back measures 18¹/₄ (18¹/₂: 18¹/₂: 18³/₄: 19: 19¹/₂)in/46 (47: 47: 48: 48: 49)cm, ending with a WS row.

Shape armholes

Keeping patt correct, bind off 8 (9: 9: 10: 10: 11) sts at beg of next 2 rows. 143 (147: 155: 159: 167: 171) sts.
Dec 1 st at each end of next 9 (9: 11: 11: 13: 13) rows, then on foll 7 (8: 8: 9: 9: 10) alt rows, then on foll 4th row. 109 (111: 115: 117: 121: 123) sts.
Work even until armhole measures 9 (9: 9¹/₂: 9¹/₂: 9³/₄: 9³/₄)in/23 (23: 24: 24: 25: 25)cm, ending with a WS row.

Shape shoulders and back neck

Bind off 10 (10: 11: 11: 11: 12) sts at beg of next 2 rows. 89 (91: 93: 95: 99: 99) sts.
Next row (RS): Bind off 10 (10: 11: 11: 11: 12) sts, patt until there are 14 (14: 14: 15: 16: 15) sts on right needle and turn, leaving rem sts on a holder.
Work each side of neck separately.
Bind off 4 sts at beg of next row.
Bind off rem 10 (10: 10: 11: 12: 11) sts.
With RS facing, rejoin yarn to rem sts, bind off center 41 (43: 43: 43: 45: 45) sts, patt to end.
Complete to match first side, reversing shapings.

FRONT

Work as given for back until 20 (22: 22: 22: 22: 22) rows less have been worked than on back to start of shoulder shaping, ending with a WS row.

Shape neck

Next row (RS): Patt 42 (43: 45: 46: 47: 48) sts and turn, leaving rem sts on a holder.
Work each side of neck separately.
Dec 1 st at neck edge of next 7 rows, then on foll 4 (5: 5: 5: 5: 5) alt rows, then on foll 4th row, ending with a WS row. 30 (30: 32: 33: 34: 35) sts.

Shape shoulder

Bind off 10 (10: 11: 11: 11: 12) sts at beg of next and foll alt row.
Work 1 row.
Bind off rem 10 (10: 10: 11: 12: 11) sts.
With RS facing, rejoin yarn to rem sts, bind off center 25 (25: 25: 25: 27: 27) sts, patt to end.
Complete to match first side, reversing shapings.

SLEEVES (both alike)

Cast on 65 (67: 67: 69: 71: 71) sts using size 2 (2³/₄mm) needles.

Row 1 (RS): (P1 tbl) 1 (2: 2: 3: 1: 1) times, *(K1 tbl) 3 times, (P1 tbl) 3 times, rep from * to last 4 (5: 5: 6: 4: 4) sts, (K1 tbl) 3 times, (P1 tbl) 1 (2: 2: 3: 1: 1) times.

Row 2: (K1 tbl) 1 (2: 2: 3: 1: 1) times, *(P1 tbl) 3 times, (K1 tbl) 3 times, rep from * to last 4 (5: 5: 6: 4: 4) sts, (P1 tbl) 3 times, (K1 tbl) 1 (2: 2: 3: 1: 1) times.

These 2 rows form twisted rib.

Cont in twisted rib for a further 28 rows, ending with a WS row.

Change to size 3 (3¼mm) needles.

Beg and ending rows as indicated and rep the 36 row patt rep throughout, cont in patt from chart, shaping sides by inc 1 st at each end of next and every foll 4th row to 79 (81: 93: 91: 99: 105) sts, then on every foll 6th row until there are 109 (111: 115: 117: 121: 123) sts, taking inc sts into patt.

Work even until sleeve measures 17½ (17½: 17½: 18: 18: 18)in/45 (45: 45: 46: 46: 46)cm, ending with a WS row.

Shape sleeve cap

Keeping patt correct, bind off 8 (9: 9: 10: 10: 11) sts at beg of next 2 rows. 93 (93: 97: 97: 101: 101) sts.

Dec 1 st at each end of next 11 rows, then on foll 7 alt rows, then on every foll 4th row until 51 (51: 55: 55: 59: 59) sts rem.

Work 1 row, ending with a WS row.
Dec 1 st at each end of next and every foll alt row to 43 sts, then on foll 7 rows, ending with a WS row.
Bind off rem 29 sts.

FINISHING
BLOCK as described on page 123.
Join right shoulder seam using backstitch, or mattress stitch if preferred.

Collar
With RS facing and using size 2 (2¾mm) needles, pick up and knit 24 (26: 26: 26: 27: 27) sts down left side of neck, 26 (26: 26: 26: 28: 28) sts from front, 24 (26: 26: 26: 27: 27) sts up right side of neck, then 49 (51: 51: 51: 53: 53) sts from back. 123 (129: 129: 129: 135: 135) sts.

Row 1 (WS): (P1 tbl) 3 times, *(K1 tbl) 3 times, (P1 tbl) 3 times, rep from * to end.

Row 2: (K1 tbl) 3 times, *(P1 tbl) 3 times, (K1 tbl) 3 times, rep from * to end.

These 2 rows form rib.

Cont in rib until collar measures 4in/10cm, ending with a WS row.

Next row (RS): (K1 tbl) 3 times, *(P1 tbl) twice, M1P, P1 tbl, (K1 tbl) 3 times, rep from * to end. 143 (150: 150: 150: 157: 157) sts.

Next row: (P1 tbl) 3 times, *(K1 tbl) 4 times, (P1 tbl) 3 times, rep from * to end.

Next row: (K1 tbl) 3 times, *(P1 tbl) 4 times, (K1 tbl) 3 times, rep from * to end.

Change to size 3 (3¼mm) needles.
Rep last 2 rows until collar measures 8¼in/21cm.
Bind off in rib.
See page 124 for finishing instructions, setting in sleeves using the set-in method.

Key ▫ K on RS, P on WS ▪ P on RS, K on WS

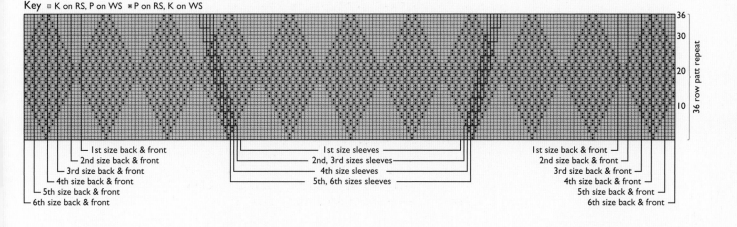

36 row patt repeat

1st size back & front
2nd size back & front
3rd size back & front
4th size back & front
5th size back & front
6th size back & front

1st size sleeves
2nd, 3rd sizes sleeves
4th size sleeves
5th, 6th sizes sleeves

1st size back & front
2nd size back & front
3rd size back & front
4th size back & front
5th size back & front
6th size back & front

RICH COLORS

This deeper color palette in autumnal shades of burgundy, plum, and mauve is sophisticated and smart, yet feminine and appealing. Flattering fluted collars abound, along with jazzy accessories, including a great looped bag and funky hat! Yarns in this section include soft mohairs and cottons.

Left *The neat, loose-fitting, hip-length Casual Sweater, knitted in stockinette stitch in a super-soft cotton, has garter-stitch cuffs and collar. (Instructions on page 112.)*

Right *The very simple, dressy Mesh Scarf is crocheted in a lightweight cotton yarn and has a fluted trim in a contrasting color. It is shown here with the Round-neck Top. (Instructions for scarf on page 122 and for top on page 78.)*

Right The Loop-collar Sweater, knitted in a cotton yarn, has a face-framing neckline with its deep rolled, loop-fringed collar and matching cuffs. It can be worn casually with jeans or dressed up for the evening. (Instructions on page 116)

Far right The Cable-rib Sweater, also knitted in cotton yarn, is a great long-length textured sweater for easy living. (Instructions on page 118.)

Left and above In a soft mohair-mix yarn, the Loop-stitch Scarf, Bag, and Hat make a great matching set and are fun to wear and to knit. Once you have mastered the looped knitting, the rest is plain sailing. (Instructions on page 114.)

Left *The Lace-ruffle Jacket is a really versatile short coat or long jacket. Ideal for wearing over smart trousers or a long skirt, it is knitted in an Aran-weight merino wool. The prettily ruffled edge, in a matching mohair/silk yarn, runs right around the front and hem. (Instructions on page 120.)*

CASUAL SWEATER

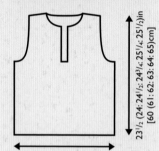

23½ (24: 24½: 24¾: 25¼: 25½)in [60 (61: 62: 63: 64: 65)cm]

20½ (21½: 22½: 24: 25: 26)in [52 (55: 57.5: 60.5: 63.5: 66)cm]

17¼ (17¼: 17¼: 17¾: 17¾: 17¾)in [44 (44: 44: 45: 45: 45)cm]

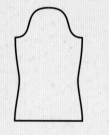

SIZES

1	2	3	4	5	6

TO FIT BUST

36	38	40	42	44	46	in
91	97	102	107	112	117	cm

YARN

Rowan Calmer—dark purple (478)

8	8	9	9	10	10 x 50g

NEEDLES

1 pair size 8 (5mm) needles
1 pair size 6 (4mm) needles

GAUGE

21 sts and 30 rows to 4in/10cm measured over St st using size 8 (5mm) needles.

BACK

Cast on 109 (115: 121: 127: 133: 139) sts using size 6 (4mm) needles.
Work in garter st for 4 rows, ending with a WS row.
Change to size 8 (5mm) needles.
Row 5 (RS): Knit.
Row 6: K3, P to last 3 sts, K3.
Rep last 2 rows 11 times, ending with a WS row.
Beg with a K row, cont in St st until back measures 14½ (15: 15: 15¼: 15½: 15¾)in/37 (38: 38: 39: 39: 40)cm, ending with a WS row.
Shape armholes
Bind off 6 (7: 7: 8: 8: 9) sts at beg of next 2 rows. 97 (101: 107: 111: 117: 121) sts.
Dec 1 st at each end of next 5 (5: 7: 7: 9: 9) rows, then on foll 3 (4: 4: 5: 5: 6) alt rows, then on every foll 4th row until 77 (79: 81: 83: 85: 87) sts rem.**
Work even until armhole measures 9 (9: 9½: 9½: 9¾: 9¾)in/23 (23: 24: 24: 25: 25)cm, ending with a WS row.
Shape shoulders and back neck
Bind off 6 (6: 7: 7: 7: 7) sts at beg of next 2 rows. 65 (67: 67: 69: 71: 73) sts.
Next row (RS): Bind off 6 (6: 7: 7: 7: 7) sts,

K until there are 11 (11: 10: 11: 11: 12) sts on right needle and turn, leaving rem sts on a holder.
Work each side of neck separately.
Bind off 4 sts at beg of next row.
Bind off rem 7 (7: 6: 7: 7: 8) sts.
With RS facing, rejoin yarn to rem sts, bind off center 31 (33: 33: 33: 35: 35) sts, K to end.
Complete to match first side, reversing shapings.

FRONT

Work as given for back to **.
***Work 3 (1: 3: 1: 3: 1) rows, ending with a WS row.
Divide for front opening
Next row (RS): K36 (37: 38: 39: 40: 41) and turn, leaving rem sts on a holder.
Work each side of neck separately.
Work even until 17 (19: 19: 19: 19: 19) rows less have been worked than on back to start of shoulder shaping, ending with a RS row.
Shape neck
Bind off 8 (8: 8: 8: 9: 9) sts at beg of next row. 28 (29: 30: 31: 31: 32) sts.
Dec 1 st at neck edge of next 6 rows, then on foll 1 (2: 2: 2: 2: 2) alt rows, then on every foll 4th row until 19 (19: 20: 21: 21: 22) sts rem, ending with a WS row.
Shape shoulder
Bind off 6 (6: 7: 7: 7: 7) sts at beg of next and foll alt row.
Work 1 row.
Bind off rem 7 (7: 6: 7: 7: 8) sts.
With RS facing, slip center 5 sts onto a holder, rejoin yarn to rem sts, K to end.
Complete to match first side, reversing shapings.

SLEEVES (both alike)

Cast on 79 (81: 81: 83: 85: 85) sts using size 6 (4mm) needles.
Work in garter st for 4 rows, ending with a WS row.
Change to size 8 (5mm) needles.
Row 5 (RS): Knit.

Row 6: K3, P to last 3 sts, K3.

Rows 7 to 10: Rep rows 5 and 6 twice.

Row 11: K3, K2tog, K to last 5 sts, skp, K3.

Row 12: Rep row 6.

Rows 13 to 16: Rep rows 5 and 6 twice.

Rep rows 11 to 16 (6 rows) twice more. 73 (75: 75: 77: 79: 79) sts.

Beg with a K row, cont in St st, dec 1 st at each end of 7th and every foll 6th row until 61 (63: 63: 65: 67: 67) sts rem.

Work 5 rows, ending with a WS row.

Inc 1 st at each end of next and every foll 6th (6th: 6th: 6th: 6th: 4th) row to 71 (73: 81: 81: 83: 73) sts, then on every foll 8th (8th: -: 8th: 8th: 6th) row until there are 77 (79: -: 83: 85: 87) sts.

Work even until sleeve measures 17¼ (17¼: 17¼: 17¾: 17¾: 17¾)in/44 (44: 44: 45: 45: 45)cm, ending with a WS row.

Shape sleeve cap

Bind off 6 (7: 7: 8: 8: 9) sts at beg of next 2 rows. 65 (65: 67: 67: 69: 69) sts.

Dec 1 st at each end of next 7 rows, then on every foll alt row to 45 sts, then on every foll 4th row until 33 sts rem.

Work 1 row, ending with a WS row.

Dec 1 st at each end of next 6 rows, ending with a WS row.

Bind off rem 21 sts.

FINISHING

BLOCK as described on page 123.

Join both shoulder seams using backstitch, or mattress stitch if preferred.

Left front border

Cast on 5 sts using size 6 (4mm) needles.

Work in garter st until border, when slightly stretched, fits up left side of front opening, from base of opening to neck shaping, ending with a WS row.

Break yarn and leave sts on a holder.

Right front border

Slip 5 sts left on holder at base of front opening onto size 6 (4mm) needles and rejoin yarn with RS facing.

Work in garter st until border, when slightly stretched, fits up right side of front opening to neck shaping, ending with a WS row.

Do NOT break yarn.

Slip stitch borders in place, sewing cast-on edge of left front border to WS behind pick-up row of right front border.

Collar

With RS facing and using size 6 (4mm) needles, K 5 sts of right front border, pick up and knit 24 (26: 26: 26: 27: 27) sts up right side of neck, 39 (41: 41: 41: 43: 43) sts from back, and 24 (26: 26: 26: 27: 27) sts down left side of neck, then K 5 sts of left front border. 97 (103: 103: 103: 107: 107) sts.

Cont in garter st until collar measures 4¾in/12cm, ending with RS of body facing for next row.

Bind off knitwise.

See page 124 for finishing instructions, setting in sleeves using the set-in method and leaving side and sleeve seams open for first 28 rows.

LOOP-STITCH SCARF & BAG

YARN
Rowan Kid Classic—lavender ice (841)
SCARF
7 x 50g
BAG
5 x 50g

NEEDLES
1 pair size 7 (4½mm) needles
Bag only: 1 pair size 6 (4mm) needles

EXTRAS—bag only: piece of lining fabric
16in x28in/40cm x 70cm; same size piece of
polyester batting; sewing thread.

GAUGE
16 sts and 25 rows to 4in/10cm measured
over pattern using size 7 (4½mm) needles.

FINISHED SIZE
Completed scarf measures 10in/26cm wide
and 71in/180cm long.
Completed bag measures 10in/26cm wide and
10in/26cm deep.

SPECIAL ABBREVIATIONS
make loop = K1 leaving st on left needle,
bring yarn to front of work between needles
and wrap it twice round thumb of left hand,

take yarn back to WS of work between
needles and K same st again, letting st slip off
left needle, bring yarn to front of work
between needles and take it back to WS over
right needle point, lift last 2 sts on right needle
over this loop and off right needle.

LOOP STITCH SCARF

TO MAKE
Cast on 41 sts using size 7 (4½mm) needles.
Row 1 (WS): Knit.
Row 2: K1, *make loop, K1, rep from * to end.
Row 3: Knit.
Row 4: K2, *make loop, K1, rep from * to last
st, K1.
These 4 rows form patt.
Cont in patt until scarf measures 71in/180cm,
ending with a RS row.
Bind off knitwise (on WS).

FINISHING
BLOCK as described on page 123.

LOOP STITCH BAG

SIDES (make 2)
Cast on 41 sts using size 7 (4½mm) needles.
**Row 1 (WS): Knit.
Row 2: K1, *make loop, K1, rep from * to end.
Row 3: Knit.
Row 4: K2, *make loop, K1, rep from * to last
st, K1.
These 4 rows form patt.
Cont in patt until side measures 9¾in/25cm,
ending with a RS row.
Change to size 6 (4mm) needles.
Work in garter st for 4 rows.
Bind off knitwise (on WS).

GUSSETS (make 2)
Cast on 17 sts using size 7 (4½mm) needles.
Complete the gusset as given for sides
from **.

BASE
Cast on 17 sts using size 7 (4½mm) needles.
Cont in patt as given for sides until base
measures 10¼in/26cm, ending with a RS row.
Bind off knitwise (on WS).

HANDLES (make 2)
Cast on 21 sts using size 6 (4mm) needles.
Row 1 (RS): K6, sLIP, K7, sLIP, K6.
Row 2: Purl.
Rep these 2 rows until handle measures
14¼in/36cm, ending with a WS row.
Bind off.

FINISHING
BLOCK as described on page 123.
From lining fabric, cut out sides, gussets and
base, adding seam allowance along all edges.
Cut out same pieces from batting and baste
wadding to WS of lining fabric pieces. Join sides
to gussets, matching cast-on and bound-off
edges. Sew base to cast-on edges. Fold handles
along slip stitch lines and join seam. Attach
ends of handles to inside of upper (bound-off)
edge of sides, positioning handles 2¾in/7cm
apart. Make up lining sections in same way as
knitted sections. Fold seam allowance to WS
around upper edge. Slip lining inside bag and
slip stitch in place around upper opening edge.

LOOP-STITCH HAT

YARN
Rowan Kid Classic—lavender ice (841)
2 x 50g

NEEDLES
1 pair size 7 (4½mm) needles

GAUGE
16 sts and 25 rows to 4in/10cm measured over pattern using size 7 (4½mm) needles.

FINISHED SIZE
Completed hat measures 20in/51cm around head.

SPECIAL ABBREVIATIONS
make loop = K1 leaving st on left needle, bring yarn to front of work between needles and wrap it twice round thumb of left hand, take yarn back to WS of work between needles and K same st again, letting st slip off left needle, bring yarn to front of work between needles and take it back to WS over right needle point, lift last 2 sts on right needle over this loop and off right needle.

HAT
Cast on 81 sts using size 7 (4½mm) needles.
Row 1 (WS): Knit.

Row 2: K1, *make loop, K1, rep from * to end.
Row 3: Knit.
Row 4: K2, *make loop, K1, rep from * to last st, K1.
These 4 rows form patt.
Cont in patt until hat measures 5in/13cm, ending with a RS row.
Shape crown
Row 1 (WS): *K8, K2tog, rep from * to last st, K1. 73 sts.
Work 1 row.
Row 3: *K7, K2tog, rep from * to last st, K1. 65 sts.
Work 1 row.
Row 5: *K6, K2tog, rep from * to last st, K1. 57 sts.
Work 1 row.
Row 7: *K5, K2tog, rep from * to last st, K1. 49 sts.
Work 1 row.
Row 9: *K4, K2tog, rep from * to last st, K1. 41 sts.
Work 1 row.
Row 11: *K3, K2tog, rep from * to last st, K1. 33 sts.
Work 1 row.
Row 13: *K2, K2tog, rep from * to last st, K1. 25 sts.
Work 1 row.
Row 15: K1, (K2tog) 12 times.
Break yarn and thread through rem 13 sts. Pull up tight and fasten off securely.

FINISHING
BLOCK as described on page 123.
Join crown and back seam.

LOOP-COLLAR SWEATER

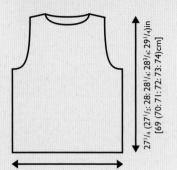

22 (23: 24: 25: 26½: 27½)in
[56 (58.5: 61.5: 64: 67: 69.5)cm]

27¼ (27½: 28: 28¼: 28¾: 29¼)in
[69 (70: 71: 72: 73: 74)cm]

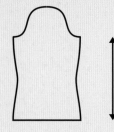

17¼ (17¼: 17¼: 17¾: 17¾: 17¾)in
[44 (44: 44: 45: 45: 45)cm]

SIZES

1	2	3	4	5	6

TO FIT BUST

| 36 | 38 | 40 | 42 | 44 | 46 | in |
| 91 | 97 | 102 | 107 | 112 | 117 | cm |

YARN

Rowan All Seasons Cotton—dark plum
(181)

16	16	17	18	18	19 x 50g

NEEDLES AND CROCHET HOOK

1 pair size 6 (4mm) needles
1 pair size 7 (4½mm) needles
Size E-4 (3.50mm) crochet hook

GAUGE

18 sts and 25 rows to 4in/10cm measured
over St st using size 7 (4½mm) needles.

CROCHET ABBREVIATIONS

ch = chain; **sc** = single crochet.

BACK

Cast on 101 (105: 111: 115: 121: 125) sts using
size 6 (4mm) needles.
Work in garter st for 4 rows, ending with a
WS row.
Change to size 7 (4½mm) needles.
Row 5 (RS): Knit.
Row 6: K4, P to last 4 sts, K4.
Rep last 2 rows 14 times more, ending with a
WS row.
Beg with a K row, cont in St st until back
measures 18¼ (18½: 18½: 19: 19: 19½)in/
46 (47: 47: 48: 48: 49)cm, ending with a
WS row.
Shape armholes
Bind off 5 (6: 6: 7: 7: 8) sts at beg of next 2
rows. 91 (93: 99: 101: 107: 109) sts.
Dec 1 st at each end of next 5 (5: 7: 7: 9: 9)
rows, then on foll 4 alt rows, then on every
foll 4th row until 69 (71: 73: 75: 77: 79)
sts rem.
Work even until armhole measures 9 (9: 9½:

9½: 9¾: 9¾)in/23 (23: 24: 24: 25: 25)cm, ending
with a WS row.
Shape shoulders and back neck
Bind off 5 (5: 5: 6: 6: 6) sts at beg of next 2
rows. 59 (61: 63: 63: 65: 67) sts.
Next row (RS): Bind off 5 (5: 5: 6: 6: 6) sts,
K until there are 9 (9: 10: 9: 9: 10) sts on right
needle and turn, leaving rem sts on a holder.
Work each side of neck separately.
Bind off 4 sts at beg of next row.
Bind off rem 5 (5: 6: 5: 5: 6) sts.
With RS facing, rejoin yarn to rem sts, bind off
center 31 (33: 33: 33: 35: 35) sts, K to end.
Complete to match first side, reversing
shapings.

FRONT

Work as given for back until 8 (10: 10: 10: 10:
10) rows less have been worked than on back
to start of shoulder shaping, ending with a
WS row.
Shape neck
Next row (RS): K24 (25: 26: 27: 27: 28) and
turn, leaving rem sts on a holder.
Work each side of neck separately.
Bind off 5 sts at beg of next row. 19 (20: 21:
22: 22: 23) sts.
Dec 1 st at neck edge of next 3 rows, then on
foll 1 (2: 2: 2: 2: 2) alt rows. 15 (15: 16: 17: 17:
18) sts.
Work 1 row, ending with a WS row.
Shape shoulder
Bind off 5 (5: 5: 6: 6: 6) sts at beg of next and
foll alt row.
Work 1 row.
Bind off rem 5 (5: 6: 5: 5: 6) sts.
With RS facing, rejoin yarn to rem sts, bind off
center 21 (21: 21: 21: 23: 23) sts, K to end.
Complete to match first side, reversing
shapings.

SLEEVES (both alike)

Cast on 67 (69: 69: 71: 73: 73) sts using size 6
(4mm) needles.
Work in garter st for 4 rows, ending with a
WS row.

Change to size 7 (4½mm) needles.
Beg with a K row, cont in St st, shaping sides by dec 1 st at each end of 9th and every foll 6th row to 59 (61: 61: 63: 65: 65) sts, then on every foll 8th row until 53 (55: 55: 57: 59: 59) sts rem.
Work 5 rows, ending with a WS row.
Inc 1 st at each end of next and every foll 4th row to 59 (61: 67: 67: 69: 75) sts, then on every foll 6th row until there are 69 (71: 73: 75: 77: 79) sts.
Work even until sleeve measures 17¼ (17¼: 17¼: 17¾: 17¾: 17¾)in/44 (44: 44: 45: 45: 45)cm, ending with a WS row.

Shape sleeve cap
Bind off 5 (6: 6: 7: 7: 8) sts at beg of next 2 rows. 59 (59: 61: 61: 63: 63) sts.
Dec 1 st at each end of next 7 rows, then on foll 4 alt rows, then on every foll 4th row until 33 (33: 35: 35: 37: 37) sts rem.
Work 1 row, ending with a WS row.
Dec 1 st at each end of next and every foll alt row to 23 sts, then on foll 3 rows, ending with a WS row.
Bind off rem 17 sts.

FINISHING
BLOCK as described on page 123.
Join both shoulder seams using backstitch, or mattress stitch if preferred.

Collar
Cast on 98 (98: 98: 98: 114: 114) sts using size 6 (4mm) needles.
Row 1 (WS): K2, *P2, K2, rep from * to end.
Row 2: P2, *K2, P2, rep from * to end.
These 2 rows form rib.
Cont in rib until collar measures 3¼in/8cm, ending with a WS row.
Next row (RS): Rib 24 (24: 24: 24: 28: 28), M1, K1, place marker on needle, K1, M1, rib 46 (46: 46: 46: 54: 54), M1, K1, place marker on needle, K1, M1, rib to end. 102 (102: 102: 102: 118: 118) sts.
Next row: *Rib to within 1 st of marker, M1, P2 (marker is between these 2 sts), M1, rep

from * once more, rib to end.
Next row: *Rib to within 1 st of marker, M1, K2 (marker is between these 2 sts), M1, rep from * once more, rib to end.
Rep last 2 rows 12 times more. 206 (206: 206: 206: 222: 222) sts.
Bind off in rib.
Join row-end edges of collar. Matching sts directly below markers to center front and back neck, sew cast-on edge of collar to neck edge.

Fringe edging
With RS facing and using size E-4 (3.50mm) crochet hook, rejoin yarn to bound-off edge of collar level with seam, ch1 (does NOT count as st), work 1 row of sc evenly around bound-off edge of collar, ending with 1 slip st in first sc.
Next round (RS): Ch1 (does NOT count as st), (1sc, ch16, 1sc) in each sc to end, 1 slip st in first sc.
Fasten off.
Join sleeve seams, then work fringe edging around lower edge of sleeves in same way.
See page 124 for finishing instructions, setting in sleeves using the set-in method and leaving side seams open for first 34 rows.

CABLE-RIB SWEATER

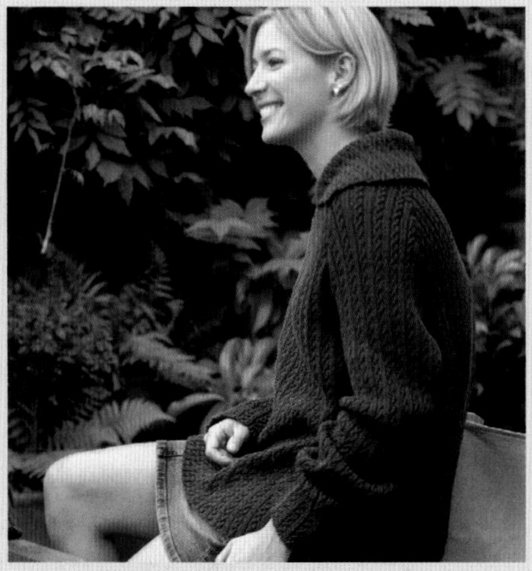

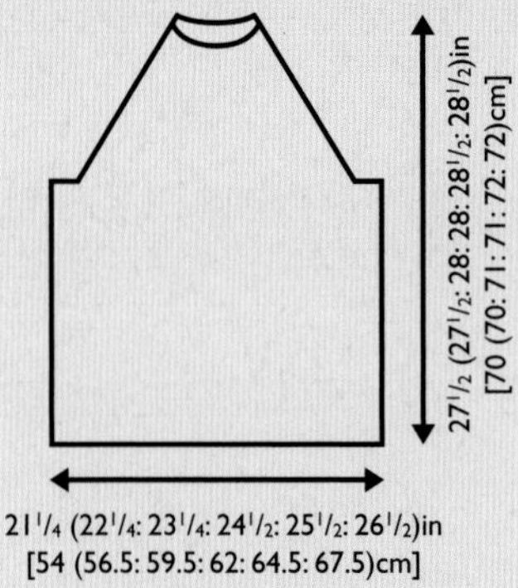
27½ (27½: 28: 28: 28½: 28½)in
[70 (70: 71: 71: 72: 72)cm]
21¼ (22¼: 23¼: 24½: 25½: 26½)in
[54 (56.5: 59.5: 62: 64.5: 67.5)cm]

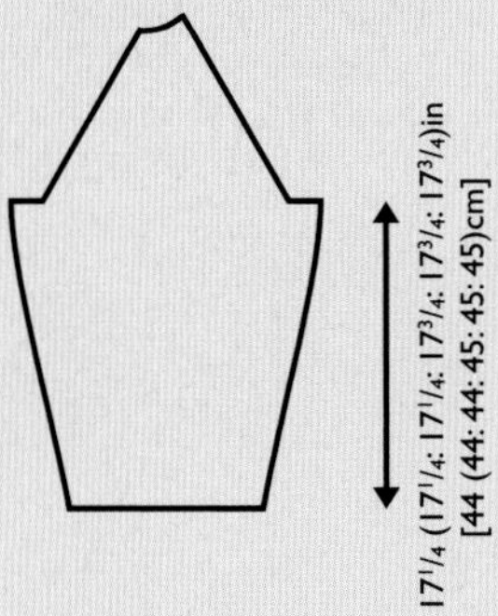
17¼ (17¼: 17¼: 17¾: 17¾: 17¾)in
[44 (44: 44: 45: 45: 45)cm]

SIZES

1	2	3	4	5	6	

TO FIT BUST

36	38	40	42	44	46	in
91	97	102	107	112	117	cm

YARN

Rowan Cotton Glace—dark plum (806)

19	19	20	21	21	22 x 50g

NEEDLES

1 pair size 2 (2¾mm) needles
1 pair size 3 (3¼mm) needles
Cable needle

GAUGE

30 sts and 36 rows to 4in/10cm measured over pattern using size 3 (3¼mm) needles.

SPECIAL ABBREVIATION

C3B = slip next 2 sts onto cable needle and leave at back of work, K1 tbl, slip the P st from cable needle back onto left needle and P this st, then K1 tbl from cable needle.

BACK

Cast on 162 (170: 178: 186: 194: 202) sts using size 2 (2¾mm) needles.

Row 1 (RS): K3 (0: 4: 1: 0: 2), (P1, K1 tbl) 0 (0: 0: 0: 2: 0) times, P0 (0: 0: 0: 1: 0), *K2, (P1, K1 tbl) twice, P1, rep from * to last 5 (2: 6: 3: 0: 4) sts, K5 (2: 6: 3: 0: 4).

Row 2: P3 (0: 4: 1: 0: 2), (K1, P1 tbl) 0 (0: 0: 0: 2: 0) times, K0 (0: 0: 0: 1: 0), *P2, (K1, P1 tbl) twice, K1, rep from * to last 5 (2: 6: 3: 0: 4) sts, P5 (2: 6: 3: 0: 4).

Row 3: K3 (0: 4: 1: 0: 2), (P1, C3B, P1) 0 (0: 0: 0: 1: 0) times, *K2, P1, C3B, P1, rep from * to last 5 (2: 6: 3: 0: 4) sts, K5 (2: 6: 3: 0: 4).

Row 4: Rep row 2.

These 4 rows form patt.

Cont in patt for a further 4 rows, ending with a WS row.

Change to size 3 (3¼mm) needles.

Cont in patt until back measures 17in/43cm, ending with a WS row.

Shape raglan armholes

Keeping patt correct, bind off 8 sts at beg of next 2 rows. 146 (154: 162: 170: 178: 186) sts.

Dec 1 st at each end of next 7 (11: 17: 23: 27: 33) rows, then on every foll alt row until 48 (50: 50: 50: 52: 52) sts rem.

Work 1 row, ending with a WS row.

Shape back neck

Next row (RS): Work 2 tog, patt 4 sts and turn, leaving rem sts on a holder.

Work each side of neck separately.

Dec 1 st at beg of next row.

Bind off rem 4 sts.

With RS facing, rejoin yarn to rem sts, bind off center 36 (38: 38: 38: 40: 40) sts, patt to last 2 sts, work 2 tog.

Complete to match first side, reversing shapings.

FRONT

Work as given for back until 66 (70: 70: 70: 72: 72) sts rem in raglan armhole shaping.

Work 1 row, ending with a WS row.

Shape neck

Next row (RS): Work 2 tog, patt 22 (24: 24: 24: 24: 24) sts and turn, leaving rem sts on a holder.

Work each side of neck separately.

Bind off 5 sts at beg of next and foll alt row and at same time dec 1 st at raglan armhole edge on 2nd row. 12 (14: 14: 14: 14: 14) sts.

Dec 1 st at each end of next and every foll alt row until 2 sts rem.

Work 1 row, ending with a WS row.

Next row (RS): K2tog and fasten off.

With RS facing, rejoin yarn to rem sts, bind off center 18 (18: 18: 18: 20: 20) sts, patt to last 2 sts, work 2 tog.

Complete to match first side, reversing shapings.

SLEEVES

Cast on 79 (81: 81: 83: 85: 85) sts using size 2 (2¾mm) needles.

Row 1 (RS): P0 (1: 1: 0: 1: 1), (K1 tbl, P1)

0 (0: 0: 1: 1: 1) times, *K2, (P1, K1 tbl) twice,
P1, rep from * to last 2 (3: 3: 4: 5: 5) sts, K2,
(P1, K1 tbl) 0 (0: 0: 1: 1: 1) times, P0 (1: 1: 0:
1: 1).

Row 2: K0 (1: 1: 0: 1: 1), (P1 tbl, K1) 0 (0: 0: 1:
1: 1) times, *P2, (K1, P1 tbl) twice, K1, rep
from * to last 2 (3: 3: 4: 5: 5) sts, P2, (K1, P1
tbl) 0 (0: 0: 1: 1: 1) times, K0 (1: 1: 0: 1: 1).

Row 3: P0 (1: 1: 0: 1: 1), (K1 tbl, P1) 0 (0: 0: 1:
1: 1) times, *K2, P1, C3B, P1, rep from * to last
2 (3: 3: 4: 5: 5) sts, K2, (P1, K1 tbl) 0 (0: 0: 1: 1:
1) times, P0 (1: 1: 0: 1: 1).

Row 4: Rep row 2.

These 4 rows form patt.

Cont in patt for a further 4 rows, inc 1 st
at each end of 3rd of these rows and
ending with a WS row. 81 (83: 83: 85: 87:
87) sts.

Change to size 3 (3¼mm) needles.

Cont in patt, shaping sides by inc 1 st at each
end of 3rd and every foll 4th row to 119 (121:
127: 125: 127: 133) sts, then on every foll 6th
row until there are 139 (141: 143: 145: 147:
149) sts, taking inc sts into patt.

Work even until sleeve measures 17¼ (17¼:
17¼: 17¾: 17¾: 17¾)in/44 (44: 44: 45: 45:
45)cm, ending with a WS row.

Shape raglan

Keeping patt correct, bind off 8 sts at beg of
next 2 rows. 123 (125: 127: 129: 131: 133) sts.

Dec 1 st at each end of next 13 rows, then on
every foll alt row until 23 sts rem.

Work 1 row, ending with a WS row.

Left sleeve only

Dec 1 st at each end of next row, then bind
off 4 sts at beg of foll row. 17 sts.

Dec 1 st at beg of next row, then bind off
5 sts at beg of foll row. 11 sts.

Rep last 2 rows once more.

Right sleeve only

Bind off 5 sts at beg and dec 1 st at end of
next row. 17 sts.

Work 1 row.

Rep last 2 rows twice more.

Both sleeves

Bind off rem 5 sts.

FINISHING

BLOCK as described on page 123.

Join both front and both back raglan seams
using backstitch, or mattress stitch if
preferred.

Collar

Cast on 172 (179: 179: 179: 186: 186) sts using
size 2 (2¾mm) needles.

Row 1 (RS): K1 tbl, P1, K1 tbl, *(P1, K1 tbl)
twice, P1, K2, rep from * to last 8 sts, (P1, K1
tbl) 4 times.

Row 2: P1 tbl, K1, P1 tbl, *(K1, P1 tbl) twice,
K1, P2, rep from * to last 8 sts, (K1, P1 tbl)
4 times.

Row 3: K1 tbl, P1, K1 tbl, *P1, C3B, P1, K2,
rep from * to last 8 sts, P1, C3B, (P1, K1 tbl)
twice.

Row 4: Rep row 2.

These 4 rows form patt.

Cont in patt until collar measures 4in/10cm,
ending with a WS row.

Change to size 3 (3¼mm) needles.

Cont in patt until collar measures 7½in/19cm,
ending with a WS row.

Bind off 17 (18: 18: 18: 19: 19) sts at beg of
next 6 rows.

Bind off rem 70 (71: 71: 71: 72: 72) sts.

See page 124 for finishing instructions.

Overlap ends of collar by 1¼in/3cm and sew
bound-off edge to neck edge, positioning
overlapped section at center front.

LACE-RUFFLE JACKET

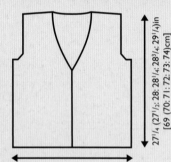

22¾ (23¾: 24½: 26: 27: 28)in
[57.5 (60.5: 62.5: 66: 68: 71)cm]

27¼ (27½: 28: 28¼: 28¾: 29¼)in
[69 (70: 71: 72: 73: 74)cm]

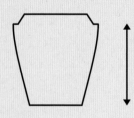

17¼ (17¼: 17¼: 17¾: 17¾: 17¾)in
[44 (44: 44: 45: 45: 45)cm]

SIZES

1	2	3	4	5	6

TO FIT BUST

36	38	40	42	44	46	in
91	97	102	107	112	117	cm

YARNS

Jaeger Extra Fine Merino Aran
A burgundy (546)

15	16	17	18	19	20 x 50g

Rowan Kidsilk Haze
B burgundy (595)

3	3	3	3	3	3 x 25g

NEEDLES

1 pair size 6 (4mm) needles
1 pair size 7 (4½mm) needles
Size 5 (3¾mm) circular needle

GAUGE

19 sts and 25 rows to 4in/10cm measured over St st using size 7 (4½mm) needles and yarn A.

BACK

Cast on 109 (115: 119: 125: 129: 135) sts using size 6 (4mm) needles and yarn A.
Row 1 (RS): K2 (0: 1: 0: 0: 0), P3 (2: 3: 1: 3: 0), *K3, P3, rep from * to last 2 (5: 1: 4: 0: 3) sts, K2 (3: 1: 3: 0: 3), P0 (2: 0: 1: 0: 0).
Row 2: P2 (0: 1: 0: 0: 0), K3 (2: 3: 1: 3: 0), *P3, K3, rep from * to last 2 (5: 1: 4: 0: 3) sts, P2 (3: 1: 3: 0: 3), K0 (2: 0: 1: 0: 0).
These 2 rows form rib.
Cont in rib for a further 12 rows, ending with a WS row.
Change to size 7 (4½mm) needles.
Beg with a K row, cont in St st until back measures 18¼ (18½: 18½: 19: 19: 19½)in/46 (47: 47: 48: 48: 49)cm, ending with a WS row.
Shape armholes
Bind off 3 sts at beg of next 2 rows. 103 (109: 113: 119: 123: 129) sts.
Dec 1 st at each end of next 6 rows. 91 (97: 101: 107: 111: 117) sts.

Work even until armhole measures 9 (9: 9½: 9½: 9¾: 9¾)in/23 (23: 24: 24: 25: 25)cm, ending with a WS row.
Shape shoulders and back neck
Bind off 10 (11: 11: 12: 13: 14) sts at beg of next 2 rows. 71 (75: 79: 83: 85: 89) sts.
Next row (RS): Bind off 10 (11: 11: 12: 13: 14) sts, K until there are 14 (14: 16: 17: 16: 17) sts on right needle and turn, leaving rem sts on a holder.
Work each side of neck separately.
Bind off 4 sts at beg of next row.
Bind off rem 10 (10: 12: 13: 12: 13) sts.
With RS facing, rejoin yarn to rem sts, bind off center 23 (25: 25: 25: 27: 27) sts, K to end.
Complete to match first side, reversing shapings.

LEFT FRONT

Cast on 55 (58: 60: 63: 65: 68) sts using size 6 (4mm) needles and yarn A.
Row 1 (RS): K2 (0: 1: 0: 0: 0), P3 (2: 3: 1: 3: 0), *K3, P3, rep from * to last 2 sts, K2.
Row 2: P2, K3, *P3, K3, rep from * to last 2 (5: 1: 4: 0: 3) sts, P2 (3: 1: 3: 0: 3), K0 (2: 0: 1: 0: 0).
These 2 rows form rib.
Cont in rib for a further 12 rows, ending with a WS row.
Change to size 7 (4½mm) needles.
Beg with a K row, cont in St st until 18 rows less have been worked than on back to beg of armhole shaping, ending with a WS row.
Shape front slope
Dec 1 st at end of next and every foll 4th row until 50 (53: 55: 58: 60: 63) sts rem.
Work 1 row, ending with a WS row.
Shape armhole
Bind off 3 sts at beg of next row. 47 (50: 52: 55: 57: 60) sts.
Work 1 row.
Dec 1 st at armhole edge of next 6 rows **and at same time** dec 1 st at front slope edge on next and foll 4th row. 39 (42: 44: 47: 49: 52) sts.
Dec 1 st at front slope edge **only** on 3rd and

every foll 4th row to 34 (34: 37: 40: 40: 43) sts, then on every foll 6th row until there are 30 (32: 34: 37: 38: 41) sts.

Work even until left front matches back to start of shoulder shaping, ending with a WS row.

Shape shoulder

Bind off 10 (11: 11: 12: 13: 14) sts at beg of next and foll alt row.

Work 1 row.

Bind off rem 10 (10: 12: 13: 12: 13) sts.

RIGHT FRONT

Cast on 55 (58: 60: 63: 65: 68) sts using size 6 (4mm) needles and yarn A.

Row 1 (RS): K2, P3, *K3, P3, rep from * to last 2 (5: 1: 4: 0: 3) sts, K2 (3: 1: 3: 0: 3), P0 (2: 0: 1: 0: 0).

Row 2: P2 (0: 1: 0: 0: 0), K3 (2: 3: 1: 3: 0), *P3, K3, rep from * to last 2 sts, P2.

These 2 rows form rib.

Complete to match left front, reversing shapings.

SLEEVES (both alike)

Cast on 53 (55: 55: 57: 59: 59) sts using size 6 (4mm) needles and yarn A.

Row 1 (RS): P1 (2: 2: 0: 1: 1), *K3, P3, rep from * to last 4 (5: 5: 3: 4: 4) sts, K3, P1 (2: 2: 0: 1: 1).

Row 2: K1 (2: 2: 0: 1: 1), *P3, K3, rep from * to last 4 (5: 5: 3: 4: 4) sts, P3, K1 (2: 2: 0: 1: 1).

These 2 rows form rib.

Cont in rib for a further 18 rows, ending with a WS row.

Change to size 7 (4½mm) needles.

Beg with a K row, cont in St st, inc 1 st at each end of next and every foll 4th row to 73 (69: 81: 75: 83: 83) sts, then on every foll 6th row until there are 87 (87: 91: 91: 95: 95) sts.

Work even until sleeve measures 17¼ (17¼: 17¼: 17¾: 17¾: 17¾)in/44 (44: 44: 45: 45: 45)cm, ending with a WS row.

Shape top of sleeve

Bind off 3 sts at beg of next 2 rows. 81 (81: 85: 85: 89: 89) sts.

Dec 1 st at each end of next and foll 4 alt rows, then on foll row, ending with a WS row.

Bind off rem 69 (69: 73: 73: 77: 77) sts.

FINISHING

BLOCK as described on page 123.

Join both shoulder seams using backstitch, or mattress stitch if preferred.

Right front band

With RS facing, using size 5 (3¾mm) circular needle and yarn B DOUBLE, starting at cast-on edge, pick up and knit 92 (94: 94: 96: 96: 98) sts up right front opening edge to start of front slope shaping, 79 (79: 81: 81: 83: 83) sts up right front slope to shoulder, then 18 (19: 20: 21: 22: 23) sts from back to center back neck. 189 (192: 195: 198: 201: 204) sts.

Row 1 (WS): K2 (1: 2: 1: 2: 1), *inc once in next st, inc twice in next st (by working into front, back, and front again of st), rep from * to last st, K1. 468 (477: 483: 492: 498: 507) sts.

Row 2: *K1, yo, K2tog, rep from * to end.

Rep row 2 until band measures 2¼in/6cm.

Bind off.

Left front band

With RS facing, using size 5 (3¾mm) circular needle and yarn B DOUBLE, starting at center back neck, pick up and knit 18 (19: 20: 21: 22: 23) sts from back to shoulder seam, 79 (79: 81: 81: 83: 83) sts down left front slope to start of front slope shaping, then 92 (94: 94: 96: 96: 98) sts down left front opening edge to cast-on edge. 189 (192: 195: 198: 201: 204) sts.

Row 1 (WS): K1, *inc twice in next st, inc once in next st, rep from * to last 2 (1: 2: 1: 2: 1) sts, K2 (1: 2: 1: 2: 1). 468 (477: 483: 492: 498: 507) sts.

Row 2: *K1, yo, K2tog, rep from * to end.

Rep row 2 until band measures 2¼in/6cm.

Bind off.

Join ends of bands at center back neck.

See page 124 for finishing instructions, setting in sleeves using the shallow set-in method.

MESH SCARF

YARN
Rowan 4 ply Cotton
A black (101)   2 x 50g
B mid dusty plum (130)   1 x 50g

CROCHET HOOK
Size B-1 (2.00mm) crochet hook

GAUGE
33 sts and 9 rows to 4in/10cm measured over
pattern using size B-1 (2.00mm) hook.

FINISHED SIZE
Completed scarf measures 6½in/17cm wide
and 69in/175cm long.

CROCHET ABBREVIATIONS
ch = chain; **tr** = treble.

SCARF
Ch60 using size B-1 (2.00mm) hook and
yarn A.
Foundation row (WS): 1tr in 9th ch from
hook, *ch2, skip 2ch, 1tr in next ch, rep from *
to end, turn. 55 sts.
Row 1: Ch6 (counts as first tr and 2ch), skip
tr at end of last row and next 2ch, *1tr in next
tr, ch2, skip 2ch, rep from * to last st, 1tr in
next ch, turn.

Last row forms patt.
Cont in patt until scarf measures 69in/175cm.
Fasten off.

FINISHING
PRESS as described on page 123.
Ruffle trim
With RS facing and using size B-1 (2.00mm)
hook, attach yarn B to base of tr at end of
row 1 and cont as foll:
Row 1 (RS): 10tr around stem of last tr of
row 1, *10tr around next 2ch of row 1, 10tr
around stem of next tr of row 1, 10tr around
next 2 foundation ch, 10tr around stem of
next tr of row 1, rep from * to end.
Fasten off.
Rejoin yarn B to base of 6ch at beg of row 2
and cont as foll:
Row 2: 10tr around 4ch at beg of row 2,
*10tr around next 2ch of row 2, 10tr around
stem of next tr of row 2, 10tr around next
2ch of row 1, 10tr around stem of next tr of
row 2, rep from * to end.
Fasten off.
In same way, work a further 2 rows of ruffles
along rows 3 and 4 of first end of scarf.
In same way, work ruffle trim along other end
of scarf.

KNITTING TECHNIQUES

Included here is information that will help you follow knitting patterns and achieve success with your knits. (See page 124 for knitting abbreviations.)

GAUGE

Obtaining the correct gauge (the correct number of stitches and rows per in/cm) will ensure a successful piece of knitting. It is especially important for knitted garments, as gauge determines both the shape and size of an article. It is recommended that you knit a square in the pattern stitch and/or stockinette stitch of perhaps 5 to 10 more stitches and 5 to 10 more rows than those given in the gauge note. Mark the central 4in/10cm square with pins and count the number or rows and stitches within this area. If you have more stitches and rows than the recommended gauge, try again using thicker needles; if you have fewer stitches and rows, try again using finer needles.

Once you have achieved the correct gauge, your garment will be knit to precisely the measurements indicated.

SIZES

In a pattern that is written for more than one size, the first figure in the set of figures for different sizes is for the smallest size and the figures for the larger sizes are inside the parentheses. When there is only one set of figures, this applies to all sizes. Be sure to follow the set of figures for your chosen size throughout. (Also, follow either the inch or centimeter measurements throughout.) If 0 (zero) or a - (hyphen) is given for your size, this instruction does not apply to your size.

When choosing which size to knit, measure one of your own garments that fits you comfortably. Having chosen an appropriate pattern size based on width, look at the corresponding length for that size; if you are not happy with the recommended length, adjust your garment before beginning the armhole shaping—any adjustment after this point will mean that the sleeve will not fit into your garment easily. Don't forget to take your adjustment into account if there is any side-seam shaping.

Finally, look at the sleeve length, taking into account any top-arm insertion length. Measure your body between the center of your neck and your wrist; this measurement should correspond to half the garment width plus the sleeve length. Again, your sleeve length may be adjusted, but remember to take into consideration your sleeve increases if you do adjust the length—you must increase more frequently than the pattern states to shorten your sleeve, less frequently to lengthen it.

CHART NOTE

Some of the patterns in this book are worked from charts. Each square on a chart represents a stitch and each line of squares a row of knitting. Each different yarn shade (or stitch instruction) used is given a color or symbol, which is shown in the key with the chart. When working from the charts, read odd rows (knit) from right to left and even rows (purl) from left to right, unless otherwise stated.

FAIR ISLE COLORWORK KNITTING

The Fair Isle technique is used when two or three colors are worked repeatedly across a row. To work this technique, strand the yarn not in use loosely across the wrong side of the knitting. If you are working with more than two colors, treat the floating yarns as if they were one yarn and always spread the stitches to their correct width to keep them elastic.

It is advisable not to carry the stranded or floating yarns over more than three stitches at a time, but to weave them under and over the color you are working, catching them into the wrong side of the work.

FINISHING INSTRUCTIONS

The pieces for your knitted garment or other projects may take hours to complete, so it would be a great pity to spoil the work by taking too little care in the blocking and finishing process. Take into account the following tips for professional-looking knits.

BLOCKING

Spread out each piece of knitting to the correct measurements and pin—this is called "blocking." Following the instructions on the yarn label, press the pieces, avoiding ribbing, garter-stitch areas, and other raised textures such as cables. Take special care to press the edges, as this will make stitching seams both easier and neater.

If the yarn label indicates that the fabric is not to be pressed, then cover the blocked out knitted fabric with a damp white cotton cloth and leave it to stand to create the desired effect.

Darn in all ends neatly along the selvage edge or a color join, as appropriate.

STITCHING SEAMS

When stitching knitted pieces together, remember to match areas of color and texture very carefully where they meet. Use a seam stitch such as backstitch or mattress stitch (an edge-to-edge stitch) for all main knitting seams. Join all ribbing (and neckbands) with mattress stitch, unless otherwise stated.

KNITTING ABBREVIATIONS

JOINING GARMENT PIECES

When stitching the seams on a knitted garment, start by joining the left shoulder and neckband seams as explained above. Then sew the top of the sleeve to the body of the garment using the method recommended in the pattern. The following are the techniques for different sleeve types.

Straight bound-off sleeves: Aligning the center of the cast-off edge of the sleeve with the shoulder seam, sew the top of the sleeve to the body, using markers as guidelines where applicable.

Square set-in sleeves: Aligning the center of the bound-off edge of the sleeve with the shoulder seam, set the top of the sleeve into the armhole so that the straight sides at the top of the sleeve form a neat right-angle with the bound-off armhole stitches on the back and front.

Shallow set-in sleeves: Aligning the center of bound-off edge of the sleeve with the shoulder seam, join the bound-off stitches at the beginning of the armhole shaping with the bound-off stitches at the start of the sleeve cap shaping. Sew the sleeve cap into the armhole, easing in the shapings.

Set-in sleeves: Aligning the center of the bound-off edge of sleeve with the shoulder seam, set in the sleeve, easing the sleeve cap into the armhole.

After joining the top of the sleeves to the back and front of the garment, join the side and sleeve seams.

Next, slip stitch any pocket edgings and linings in place, and sew on buttons to correspond with buttonholes.

Lastly, press seams, avoiding ribbing and any areas of garter stitch.

The following abbreviations are used for the patterns in this book. Explanations for special abbreviations are given with the patterns.

alt	alternate
approx	approximately
beg	begin(ning)
cm	centimeter(s)
cont	continu(e)(ing)
dec	decreas(e)(ing)
foll	follow(s)(ing)
garter st	K every row
in	inch(es)
inc	increas(e)(ing); in a row instruction work into front and back of stitch
K	knit
m	meter(s)
M1	make one stitch by picking up horizontal loop before next stitch and knitting into back of it
M1P	make one stitch by picking up horizontal loop before next stitch and purling into back of it
meas	measures
mm	millimeter(s)
oz	ounce(s)
P	purl
patt	pattern
psso	pass slipped stitch over
p2sso	pass 2 slipped stitches over
rem	remain(s)(ing)
rep	repeat(ing)
rev St st	reverse stockinette stitch (P all RS rows, K all WS rows)
RS	right side(s)
skp	slip one, knit one, pass slipped stitch over
sl 1	slip one stitch
sLIK	slip one knitwise
sLIP	slip one purlwise
st(s)	stitch(es)
St st	stockinette stitch (K all RS rows, P all WS rows)
tbl	through back of loop(s)
tog	together
WS	wrong side(s)
yd	yard(s)
yo	yarn over right-hand needle

(also known as yfwd) to make a new stitch

CROCHET TERMS

U.S. crochet terms and abbreviations have been for the crochet instructions in this book. This can cause confusion if you are used to following U.K. crochet patterns. The list below gives the U.K. equivalent where the terms vary.

U.S.	U.K.
chain (ch)	chain (ch)
slip stitch (slip st)	slip stitch (ss)
single crochet (sc)	single crochet (dc)
half double (hdc)	half treble (htr)
double crochet (dc)	treble (tr)
treble (tr)	double treble (dtr)
double treble (dtr)	triple treble (trtr)
triple treble (trtr)	quadruple treble (qtr)
skip	miss
yarn over hook (yo)	yarn over hook (yoh)

YARN INFORMATION

The following list covers the Rowan and Jaeger yarns used in this book. All the information was correct at the time of publication, but yarn companies change their products frequently and cannot absolutely guarantee that the shades or yarn types used will be available when you come to use these patterns.

For the best results, always use the yarn specified in the knitting pattern. Contact the distributors on page 126 to find a supplier of Rowan or Jaeger yarn near you. For countries not listed, contact the main office in the U.K.

The yarn descriptions here will help you find a substitute if necessary. When substituting yarn, always remember to calculate the yarn amount needed by ball length rather than by ball weight.

Note: Always check the yarn label for care instructions.

JAEGER EXTRA FINE MERINO ARAN

An Aran-weight wool yarn; 100 percent merino wool; approx 95yd/87m per 1¾oz/50g ball; 19 sts and 25 rows to 4in/10cm measured over St st using size 7 (4½mm) needles.

JAEGER EXTRA FINE MERINO CHUNKY

An chunky-weight wool yarn; 100 percent merino wool; approx 69yd/63m per 1¾oz/50g ball; 15 sts and 20 rows to 4in/10cm measured over St st using size 10 (6mm) needles.

JAEGER EXTRA FINE MERINO DK

An medium-weight wool yarn; 100 percent extra-fine merino wool; approx 137yd/125m per 1¾oz/50g ball; 22 sts and 30–32 rows to 4in/10cm measured over St st using sizes 5–6 (3¾–4mm) needles.

ROWAN ALL SEASON COTTON

A medium-weight cotton-mix yarn; 60 percent cotton, 40 percent acrylic/microfiber; approx 99yd/90m per 1¾oz/50g ball; 16–18 sts and 23–25 rows to 4in/10cm measured over St st using sizes 7–9 (4½–5½mm) needles.

ROWAN CALMER

A medium-weight cotton-mix yarn; 75 percent cotton, 25 percent acrylic/microfiber; approx 175yd/160m per 1¾oz/50g ball; 21 sts and 30 rows to 4in/10cm measured over St st using size 8 (5mm) needles.

ROWAN COTTON GLACE

A lightweight cotton yarn; 100 percent cotton; approx 126yd/115m per 1¾oz/50g ball; 23 sts and 32 rows to 4in/10cm measured over St st using sizes 3–5 (3¼–3¾mm) needles.

ROWAN DENIM

A medium-weight cotton yarn; 100 percent cotton; approx 102yd/93m per 1¾oz/50g ball; 20 sts and 28 rows (before washing) and 20 sts and 32 rows (after washing) to 4in/10cm measured over St st using size 6 (4mm) needles.

ROWAN 4PLY COTTON

A lightweight cotton yarn; 100 percent cotton; approx 186yd/170m per 1¾oz/50g ball; 27–29 sts and 37–39 rows to 4in/10cm measured over St st using sizes 2–3 (3–3¼mm) needles.

ROWAN 4PLY SOFT

A lightweight wool yarn; 100 percent merino wool; approx 191yd/175m per 1¾oz/50g ball; 28 sts and 36 rows to 4in/10cm measured over St st using size 3 (3¼mm) needles.

ROWAN KID CLASSIC

A medium-weight mohair-mix yarn; 70 percent lambswool, 26 percent kid mohair, 4 percent nylon; approx 153yd/140m per 1¾oz/50g ball; 18–19 sts and 23–25 rows to 4in/10cm measured over St st using sizes 8–9 (5–5½mm) needles.

ROWAN KIDSILK HAZE

A lightweight mohair-mix yarn; 70 percent super kid mohair, 30 percent silk; approx 229yd/210m per 1oz/25g ball; 18–25 sts and 23–34 rows to 4in/10cm measured over St st using sizes 3–8 (3¼–5mm) needles.

ROWAN PLAID

A chunky-weight wool-mix yarn; 42 percent merino wool, 30 percent acrylic fiber, 28 percent superfine alpaca; approx 109yd/100m per 3½oz/100g ball; 11–12 sts and 14–16 rows to 4in/10cm measured over St st using size 11 (8mm) needles

ROWAN AND JAEGER YARN ADDRESSES

U.S.A.
Rowan USA, c/o Westminster Fibers Inc.,
4 Townsend West, Suite 8, Nashua, NH 03063.
Tel: +1 (603) 886 5041/5043.
E-mail: rowan@westminsterfibers.com

AUSTRALIA
Australian Country Spinners, 314 Albert Street,
Brunswick, Victoria 3056. Tel: (03) 9380 3888.

BELGIUM
Pavan, Meerlaanstraat 73, B9860 Balegem
(Oosterzele). Tel: (32) 9 221 8594.
E-mail: pavan@pandora.be

CANADA
Diamond Yarn, 9697 St Laurent, Montreal,
Quebec, H3L 2N1. Tel: (514) 388 6188.
Diamond Yarn (Toronto), 155 Martin Ross,
Unit 3, Toronto, Ontario M3J 2L9.
Tel: (416) 736 6111.
www.diamondyarns.com
E-mail: diamond@diamondyarn.com

DENMARK
Designvaerkstedet, Boulevarden 9, Aalborg
9000. Tel: (45) 9812 0713. Fax: (45) 9813 0213.
Inger's, Volden 19, Aarhus 8000.
Tel: (45) 8619 4044.
Sommerfuglen, Vandkunsten 3,
Kobenhaven K 1467. Tel: (45) 3332 8290.
E-mail: mail@sommerfuglen.dk
www.sommerfuglen.dk
Uldstedet, Fiolstraede 13, Kobenhavn K 1171.
Tel/Fax: (45) 3391 1771.
Uldstedet, G1. Jernbanevej 7, Lyngby 2800.
Tel/Fax: (45) 4588 1088.
Garnhoekeren, Karen Olsdatterstraede 9,
Roskilde 4000. Tel/Fax: (45) 4637 2063.

FRANCE
Elle Tricot, 8 Rue du Coq, 67000 Strasbourg.
Tel: (33) 3 88 23 03 13.
E-mail: elletricot@agat.net
elletricot@agat.net. www.elletricote.com

GERMANY
Wolle & Design, Wolfshovener Strasse 76,
52428 Julich-Stetternich. Tel: (49) 2461 54735.
www.wolleunddesign.de
E-mail: Info@wolleunddesign.de

HOLLAND
de Afstap, Oude Leliestraat 12, 1015 AW
Amsterdam. Tel: (31) 20 6231445.

HONG KONG
East Unity Co. Ltd., Unit B2, 7/F Block B, Kailey
Industrial Centre, 12 Fung Yip Street, Chai Wan.
Tel: (852) 2869 7110. Fax (852) 2537 6952.
E-mail: eastuni@netvigator.com

ICELAND
Storkurinn, Laugavegi 59, 101 Reykjavik.
Tel: (354) 551 8258. Fax: (354) 562 8252.
E-mail: malin@mmedia.is

JAPAN
Puppy Co Ltd, T151-0051, 3-16-5 Sendagaya,
Shibuyaku, Tokyo. Tel: (81) 3 3490 2827.
E-mail: info@rowan-jaeger.com

KOREA
De Win Co Ltd, Chongam Bldg, 101,
34-7 Samsung-dong, Seoul. Tel: (82) 2 511 1087.
E-mail: knittking@yahoo.co.kr www.dewin.co.kr
My Knit Studio, (3F) 121 Kwan Hoon Dong,
Chongro-ku, Seoul. Tel: (82) 2 722 0006.
E-mail : myknit@myknit.com

NEW ZEALAND
Alterknitives, P.O. Box 47961, Ponsonby,
Auckland. Tel: (64) 9 376 0337.
E-mail: knitit@ihug.co.nz
Knit World, P.O. Box 30 645, Lower Hutt.
Tel: (64) 4 586 4530.
E-mail: knitting@xtra.co.nz
The Stitchery, Shop 8, Suncourt Shopping
Centre, 1111 Taupo. Tel: (64) 7 378 9195.

NORWAY
Paa Pinne, Tennisvn 3D, 0777 Oslo.
Tel: (47) 909 62 818.
www.paapinne.no
E-mail: design@paapinne.no

SPAIN
Oyambre, Pau Claris 145, 80009 Barcelona.
Tel: (34) 670 011957.
E-mail : comercial@oyambreonline.com

SWEDEN
Wincent, Norrtullsgatan 65, 113 45 Stockholm.
Tel: (46) 8 33 70 60.
E-mail: wincent@chello.se www.wincent.nu

U.K.
Rowan Yarns, Green Lane Mill, Holmfirth,
West Yorkshire HD9 2DX, England.
Tel: +44 (0) 1484 681 881.
Fax: +44 (0) 1484 687 920.
www.knitrowan.com

ACKNOWLEDGMENTS

Authors' acknowledgments

We would like to thank:

Kate Buller for giving us the opportunity to create this book; the team at Rowan for their great support; Sue Whiting and Stella Smith for the hours spent writing and checking the patterns; Susan Berry, Georgina Rhodes, Peter Williams, and the models for turning the concept into a visual reality; and Sally Harding for her editing skills.

Martin Storey would also like to specially thank: Mark, for his steadfast support, my mother Margaret, my sister Linda, Aunty Bette, and Aunty Pix for their patience in teaching me the joys of the craft of hand knitting.

Sharon Brant would also like to specially thank: All the knitters: Mrs Oakes, Mary, Joy, Gilly, Betty, Ruby, Heather, Elaine, Peggy, Dodie, Anna, and Eleanor for her crochet expertise. My mum, Thelma, for all the hours and patience in finishing the garments and for always being there.

Publishers' acknowledgments

We would like to thank: the models, Marian Sharp, Jan Plackett, Molly Haskey, Bluebell Martin, Poppy Martin, Kristy Jones, and Sally Turnbull for their enthusiasm and sense of fun. Julia Griffiths for her generosity, advice, and location. Carol Greenfield and Patricia Soper for taking care of hair and make-up. Lenka Paskuova and Chloe Palmer for being great assistants.